PUNCTUATIO
a simplified approach
Third Edition

W.E. Perkins, Ed.D.

Professor of Business Education
College of Education
University of North Texas

EB17CB
PUBLISHED BY
SOUTH-WESTERN PUBLISHING CO.
CINCINNATI   WEST CHICAGO, IL   CARROLLTON, TX   LIVERMORE, CA

TABLE OF CONTENTS

▶▶ PROGRAM OBJECTIVES

Have you ever wondered how much better you would feel if you could punctuate a business document with confidence? If you are like most people, you realize that your punctuation skills aren't what they should be. However, you have continued to muddle along hoping that no one will notice. Some people haven't noticed because they don't know what is correct or incorrect. Other people have noticed, though: well-educated people, friends, and employers!

This text will help you overcome the fear that your writing reveals that you lack knowledge of basic punctuation rules. Your punctuation skills can be noticeably improved if you will supply the needed ingredients: a strong desire to learn and a motivation to complete this program. By working through this text-workbook, you will learn to do the following:

1. Punctuate effectively by reviewing and working with the basic rules of punctuation.
2. Apply punctuation rules to typical business correspondence in less time and with minimum effort by setting your own learning pace.
3. Assume responsibility for your own instruction and use the skills of the teacher for diagnostic and prescribing purposes.

An educational program can be judged only on the basis of how effective it is in changing behavior. The question to answer is, "What will I be able to do after completing this text that I could not do before?" The following specific objectives will give you a good idea of what you can expect:

1. Demonstrate a marked improvement in written transcripts by a one-half reduction in punctuation errors.
2. Make from 45 percent to 60 percent fewer errors on the posttest than on the pretest.

▶▶ FEATURES AND ORGANIZATION

Research has shown that a few major basic punctuation rules cover over 98 percent of all punctuation used in business writing. For this reason, you will not be asked to learn all punctuation rules—only the ones that occur so frequently that a lack of knowledge could cause frustration. If you can master the 27 high-frequency rules, you can look up in a reference manual the 2 percent about which you are not sure.

This text-workbook has been organized into seven sections. Each section contains approximately 50 to 100 frames that teach the basic rules and permit you to practice until you understand the applications. Feedback frames are provided at the end of each section. These should be removed and placed alongside the instructional frame with which you are working so that you can immediately check the correctness of your answers *after* you have made the written responses called for. Some teachers may prefer that you wait until a whole section has been completed before any checking is done. Whichever way you work the materials, the important thing is that you make an overt response; that is, you actually write out what the directions tell you to do before checking the correct answers.

A section test—a business letter, a business memo, or a letter/memo report—is provided at the end of each of the seven sections. Each of these self-checks is simply a comprehensive review of everything you have learned up to that point. Again, the answers are provided along with a detailed number referral system that will help you review any items you missed before continuing to the next section.

►► LEARNING AIDS

In addition to the feedback frames, which are located at the end of each section, and the intensive review pages following each section test, several other aids have been added to *Punctuation: A Simplified Approach* to facilitate your study of the basic punctuation rules:

1. A complete table of contents (Easy Reference) with corresponding frame numbers has been provided for the location of each rule.
2. The instructional frame for each of the 27 basic rules has been visibly marked throughout the text with the appropriate rule number.
3. Each section opener page has the basic rules listed as well as the supplementary usage presented in that section.
4. All section review sheets (at the end of every section) have a "practice sentence line," which allows you to write a sentence of your own for each punctuation mark missed in that section test.

►► TESTS

Several tests are used in *Punctuation: A Simplified Approach* to assure that you have adequate opportunity to demonstrate that you have learned the basic rules. First, a pretest consisting of six unpunctuated business letters will be administered to you by your teacher. This pretest will be used as a basis for determining growth. Second, a section test at the end of each of the seven sections will give you feedback as to how well you are comprehending the material up to that point. And finally, a posttest—again, a battery of six unpunctuated business letters—will be given to you by your teacher. All of these tests are necessary to allow you to demonstrate your greatly improved punctuation skills.

►► HOW TO PROCEED

Please read each of the following steps and proceed accordingly:

1. If your teacher permits, tear out the feedback frames at the end of each section so that you can obtain immediate feedback on the accuracy of your responses.
2. Read each frame carefully and do exactly what the directions say.
3. Record all your responses in pencil in this text-workbook.
4. Cover the answers on the feedback frames with a sheet of paper or preferably a 5″ × 8″ card. (It is very important, of course, that you do not look at the answers until *after* you have made your response.) If there are several responses to a frame, do all of them before checking. Be sure to keep the answers covered while you are working. After you have recorded your answers in the spaces provided, move the sheet of paper or card down the page and check to see if you are right. Complete each frame in this manner.
5. Read each feedback frame carefully. Not only is the answer given, but many times the reason for the punctuation is also stated.
6. Work as rapidly as possible. If you are getting most of the exercises right, speed up even more. When you begin missing items, this will be a clue to you to slow down. Pace yourself so that you can get nine out of ten frames correct. Reread and rework certain parts if necessary to maintain this 90 per cent accuracy rate.

7. At the end of the section, read the instructions for taking the section test. After you have punctuated the entire document, turn the page and check each punctuation mark. For each numbered mark you miss, turn to the review sheets that follow and locate the frame number where that particular rule is discussed. Review the rule, and on the blank line provided, write an original sentence using any marks of punctuation that you missed. If you can construct sentences of your own using the punctuation marks that you missed, you will be more likely to correct your weaknesses before moving ahead.

8. Proceed to the next section and continue the reading-responding-checking process.

9. Ask your teacher to give you the final exam—a posttest battery of six unpunctuated business letters.

1. Use a *PERIOD* at the end of (a) a declarative sentence or (b) an imperative sentence.

2. Use a *QUESTION MARK* after a direct question.

3. Use a *PERIOD* after (a) an abbreviation which stands for a single word and (b) an abbreviation and/or initials of a proper name.

4. Use a *PERIOD* to separate (a) a whole number from a decimal fraction and (b) dollars from cents.

5. Use a *PERIOD* at the end of a sentence embodying a polite request in the form of a question.

6. Use a *COMMA* to set off digits in groups where numbers consist of four or more digits (except in series numbers).

7. Use a *COMMA* after (a) each element except the last or (b) each pair of elements except the last in a series of coordinating nouns, adjectives, verbs, or adverbs.

8. Use a *COMMA* to set off a year date that is used to explain a preceding date of the month.

9. Use a *COMMA* to set off the name of a state when the name of a city precedes it.

10. Use a *COMMA* to set off titles and degrees following a person's name.

11. Use a *COMMA* to set off *Inc.* and *Ltd.* following the name of a company.

12. Use a *COMMA* to follow the complimentary close of a letter with mixed punctuation.

13. Use a *COLON* after a salutation in a business letter with mixed punctuation.

14. Use a *COMMA* to set off a dependent (subordinate) clause that has been transposed or placed out of order in the sentence.

15. Use a *COMMA* to set off a parenthetical expression (word, phrase, or clause) when the degree of separation is not great enough to require the use of parentheses or dashes.

16. Use a *COMMA* after introductory expressions, such as *of course, however, accordingly, after all, therefore,* when they are used as conjunctions at the beginning of a sentence, in order to make a distinction between the thought that precedes and the thought that follows the expression.

*Reprinted from Donald G. Stather, "The Application of the Rules of Punctuation in Typical Business Correspondence" (Doctoral Dissertation, Boston University, 1960).

17. Use a *COMMA* to set off words or phrases that explain a preceding noun (appositives).

18. Use a *COMMA* to set off a nonrestrictive clause or phrase.

19. Use a *COMMA* to separate two or more independent (coordinate) clauses when they are joined by nor, or, and, or but.

20. Use a *SEMICOLON* to separate the independent clauses of a compound sentence when either one or both clauses are punctuated by one or more commas.

21. Use a *SEMICOLON* to separate independent clauses closely connected in meaning and not joined by a conjunction.

22. Use an *APOSTROPHE* to indicate contractions of words.

23. Use an *APOSTROPHE* to show singular or plural possessive.

24. Use *QUOTATION MARKS* to set off (a) words or phrases that are intended to be emphasized; (b) slang or coined words or phrases which might cheapen the text if it were not known that the writer is aware of them; (c) a word or phrase intended to be awkward, whimsical, or humorous; (d) a word or phrase if the expression *so-called* can be mentally supplied before it; or (e) a technical trade name.

25. Uses a *COLON* to separate hours and minutes in indicating time.

26. Use a *COLON* following the expression *as follows* used to introduce enumerations, tabulations, or long quotations.

27. Use a *HYPHEN* when two or more words have the force of a single modifier before a noun.

EASY REFERENCE

SECTION 1 (Frames 1–48)

SECTION 2 (Frames 49–149)

SECTION 3 (Frames 150–244)

SECTION 4 (Frames 245–303)

(Continued on the next page)

xi

SECTION 5 (Frames 304–384)

SECTION 6 (Frames 385–444)

Section 1

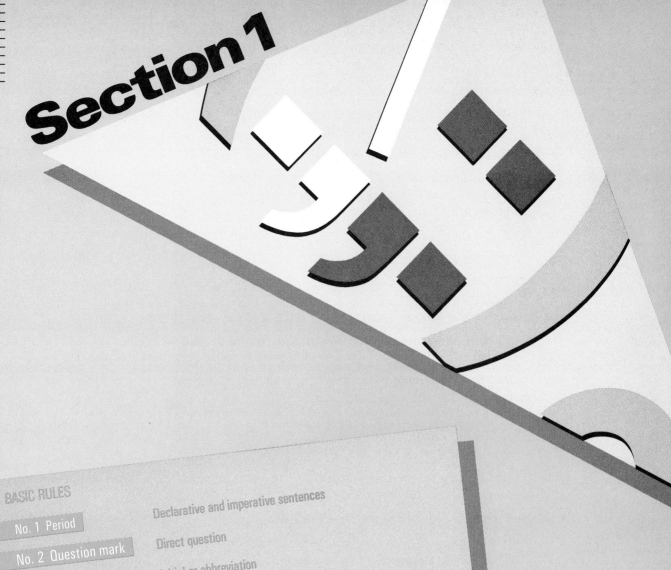

1

A **sentence** is a group of words that express a complete thought. To be complete, a sentence must contain both a subject and a verb.

Circle the letter of each complete sentence below:

    A. Nearly all of us at one time or another
    B. The decision to buy stocks should be made carefully
    C. Before making any decisions

2

Rule No. 1

Use a period at the end of a sentence that states a fact or gives a command.

    Ex.: 1. More and more women are operating businesses for themselves.
          2. Tell any callers that I am out of the office for the remainder of the day.

Example 1 is a statement of _____.
Example 2 is a _____.

3

A **declarative sentence** makes a statement of fact or states something. An **imperative sentence** gives an order, makes a command, or requests someone to do something.

Circle the letter of each declarative sentence below:

    A. Only 23 percent of all families operate from a planned budget.
    B. Mutual funds are managed by companies that receive money from many investors.
    C. Don't smoke during an interview even if the interviewer says you may do so.

4

Both declarative and imperative sentences require the use of a period as the terminal mark of punctuation. In keyboarded material two spaces follow a period at the end of a sentence.

Punctuate these complete sentences:

    A. Open a savings account with First Federal Savings before next Friday__
    B. The total dollar value of all goods and services produced in a given year is called the gross national product (GNP)__

5

Punctuate these items:

    A. Because an IRA is considered a retirement plan__
    B. Most of the new jobs created today are the result of newly formed small businesses__
    C. Municipal bonds: bonds issued by city and state governments__
    D. Anyone who provides financial support for another person probably should have life insurance__

Sometimes a period is not a strong enough mark of punctuation to end a sentence. When a writer wants to show strong emotion or emphasis, an <u>exclamation point</u> is used.

Punctuate the following sentence as you interpret the emphasis:

Run for your life__

▶ 6

An exclamation at the beginning of a sentence is an **interjection.** An interjection may or may not be a complete thought (sentence). Interjections usually require an exclamation point because of the emotion they reflect. Two spaces follow an interjection or an exclamation point at the end of a sentence.

Punctuate these sentences:

A. Great__ You are now on your way to bigger and bigger profits__
B. Give me a break__ You can't expect me to work on Sundays for only minimum wage__

▶ 7

Punctuate these sentences with a period or an exclamation point:

A. More than half of all small businesses fail within five years__
B. Terrific__ You finally understand the difference between preferred and common stocks__

▶ 8

Punctuate these items:

A. The difference between success and failure is persistence__
B. As you examine the quality of a product__
C. The richest 20 percent of the population receives about 43 percent of all income—a fact that shows the gap between rich and poor is widening__

▶ 9

Rule No. 2

Use a question mark after a direct question that requires an answer. Use a period after an indirect question that requires no answer. Two spaces follow both marks of punctuation.

Ex.: 1. How does society deal with scarcity?
2. I often wonder how much money I would need in savings in order to feel financially secure.

▶ 10

Example 1 asks a(n) _____ question.
Example 2 asks a(n) _____ question.

11

Circle the letter of the sentence that is a direct question:

  A. People commonly ask if generic brands are as good as name brands
  B. Can you explain the relationship between productivity and wages

12

Circle the letter of the sentence that is a direct question:

  A. What should be the basis for determining an individual's tax bracket
  B. José wanted to know what should be the basis for determining an individual's tax bracket

13

Punctuate these sentences:

  A. For whom should goods and services be produced___
  B. The professor was asked what the difference between a country's exports and total imports is called___

14

Punctuate these items:

  A. As a child she always wondered how a business decides what price to charge for a product or service___
  B. If you have the money, shouldn't you be able to buy anything you want___
  C. A net worth that increases from year to year___

Rule No. 3

Use a period after an initial and after most abbreviations. One space follows the period after an initial. Some abbreviations require a space following the completed abbreviation.

15

  Ex.: 1. Gabriele Albiano, M.D.
       2. Mr. Ying Wu
       3. Gustav M. Adler, Sr.
       4. Miss Clarice Chenault

M.D. stands for _____.
Mr. stands for _____.
M. stands for _____.
Sr. stands for _____.
Miss stands for _____.

4

Place a period at the end of each abbreviation in the following phrases, and draw an arrow to the point where a space would be required:

A. At 8:30 a m the pilot
B. A Ph D degree
C. equipment, i e , computers
D. Nos 17, 19, 23

16

When three or more abbreviations occur together (consecutively), the periods are frequently omitted.

Ex.: 1. U.S.A. or USA
  2. I.B.M. or IBM
  3. J.F.K. or JFK
  4. F.I.C.A. or FICA

Circle a letter below to indicate which abbreviations can be written without periods:

A. Y.M.C.A.
B. 500 B.C.

17

If an abbreviation occurs at the end of a sentence, <u>do not</u> use two periods together.

Is the following sentence punctuated correctly? _____
  (Yes/No)

  Central planners establish plans for five years at a time in the U.S.S.R..

18

Question marks and exclamation points *do* follow a period in an abbreviation at the end of a sentence.

Ex.: 1. **When did Carlos earn his M.A.?**
  2. **Mrs. Olsen demanded <u>not</u> to be addressed as Ms.!**

Insert the correct punctuation at the points indicated in the sentences below:

A. Wm__ Rinehardt, Jr__ , was born at 5:12 a__m__
B. When did Ms__ Lucretia Granger hear from the I__R__S__

19

Many businesses, professional associations, institutions, and government agencies omit periods after the abbreviations of their names. This is the option of the particular organization. References to the organization should match the company preference.

  Is this abbreviation correct? UCLA _____
  (Yes/No)

20

21

Circle the preferred abbreviation in each pair below:

A. COBOL/C.O.B.O.L.
B. NO 36/No. 36
C. A.F.L.-C.I.O./AFL-CIO
D. A.A.A./AAA
E. Phoenix, Az. 80568-1042/Phoenix, AZ 85068-1042

22

Complete the following sentence by circling the letter of the best answer below:

When writing an abbreviated name, such as NASA or UPI, you can omit the periods after each abbreviation if:

A. you are handwriting instead of keyboarding.
B. the abbreviation is three letters or more.
C. the organization writes its own name without the periods.
D. two or more reference sources indicate that omitted periods is correct.

23

Punctuate these sentences by inserting the necessary periods, exclamation points, and question marks. (Watch for periods after abbreviations, especially those followed by commas.)

A. About 70 percent of U S businesses are sole proprietorships according to Mr C N Velez
B. Why did Miss Jennifer Clayton transfer her property, which is located at 119 S Orion Place, to Dr G O Valdez, Sr

24

Punctuate these sentences:

A. What   How could Fiber Optics Industries and Chas E Spiner Corp get dropped from the AMEX in Chicago
B. Send all inquiries to: Ling Bros, Inc, 9494 E Hamilton Dr, Jackson, MS 39209-4777

Rule No. 4

Use a period to separate whole numbers from decimal fractions and dollars from cents.

Ex.: 1. Typically an entrepreneur averages 3.8 failures before the final success.
2. Her allowance was $16.75 per week, up from $14.50 the year before.

25 ▶

In Example 1 a period is used in the figure 3.8 to distinguish the whole number from the _____. In Example 2 a period is inserted in the amounts of $16.75 and $14.50 to separate _____ from _____.

No space should follow the period in decimal fractions nor in dollars and cents.

Ex.:   8.25 times $80.95   <u>not</u>   8. 25 times $80. 95

26 ▶

In each of the blanks below, write the correct amounts indicated in parentheses:

A. Around _____ (decimal point seven) of American consumers use an average of _____ (five decimal point two) credit cards.
B. Of the _____ (forty-two dollars and seventy-five cents) grocery bill, _____ (twenty-eight dollars and thirty cents) was for household supplies.

Even amounts of money (dollars with no cents) are written with no zeros and no decimal point. The decimal point and zeros are usually unnecessary.

Ex.: 1. $53   <u>not</u> $53.00   <u>nor</u> $53.
2. $10   <u>not</u> $10.00   <u>nor</u> $10.

27 ▶

Underscore the correct figure in the following sentence:

The average charity contribution was close to ($35.00/$35./$35) for every man, woman, and child.

Underscore the <u>unnecessary</u> decimals and zeros in these sentences:

A. Suppose Jesse Garza's check for $27.00 were lost or stolen.
B. At an annual percentage rate of 18 percent, the monthly interest on the credit card amounted to $66.30.
C. The 5 percent increase in utilities resulted in a $4. increase in this month's electric bill.
D. The discount made the sale price of the shrubs only $14.

28 ▶

If even and uneven amounts of money occur within the same sentence or paragraph, all <u>related</u> amounts are written with periods and zeros for consistency.

> **Ex.: Pat's interest from his savings account grew to $14.65 in March, $17.80 in April, and $20.<u>00</u> in May.**

29

Circle the letter of each correct sentence:

A. During the last three quarters, the price per bushel of wheat was as follows: $4.20, $4.00, and $3.00.

B. Gasoline prices ranged from $.87 to $1.

In the following sentences, underscore the <u>unnecessary</u> decimal and zeros in the amounts (dollars and cents):

A. During our fall sale, shoes that once sold for $39.95 are now $29.00.

B. If you multiplied $16.00 times 40 shares less a $50 discount, you would arrive at a final price of $590.00.

30

C. Few consumers purchase enough table salt to know whether it is $.50 a pound, $1.00 a pound, or $1.50 a pound.

D. Mr. Santos earns $13.00 an hour, making his earnings $28,080.00 annually.

Punctuate the following sentences:

A. To convert feet into meters, multiply by 03 (zero decimal point three); for yards, multiply by 09 (zero decimal point nine).

31

B. That company converted our order for 1775 (seventeen decimal point seventy-five) yds of wire to the metric equivalent, 1598 (fifteen decimal point ninety-eight) m

Rule No. 5

Use a period after a polite request which is stated in question form but calls for specific action rather than an answer.

> **Ex.: Could you please send us your check by June 1.**

32

Does the above example call for action or for an answer to the question?

_____
(Action/Answer)

Some statements, although in question form, are actually commands and require no direct answer. Such statements request (command) the person to take a specific action rather than to answer the question directly. These statements are called **polite requests.**

33

A polite request (does/does not) require a direct answer to the question.

Circle the letter of the polite request:

A. May we hear from you soon regarding the impending deadline__
B. When will we hear from you__

Circle a letter below to complete the following sentence correctly:

Even though a statement may appear to be a question, use a period at the end if the sentence is:

A. stated in question form.
B. long and complex.
C. a request requiring action rather than a specific answer.
D. an imperative sentence.

Read the following sentence and select the correct responses below:

Why haven't we heard from you concerning your overdue account__

The above statement is a (question/polite request) because it (does/does not) ask a direct question requiring an answer. The end punctuation mark should be a (period/question mark).

If a request in question form is a command, there is no option for refusal. Use a period rather than a question mark at the end of such statements.

Ex.: 1. **Would you please be quiet.**
     2. **Would you please be quiet?**

Which of the above examples gives no choice except "to be quiet?"

_____
(No. 1/No. 2)

Place a period after the statement which implies no choice in refusing the request:

A. Would you please come to my office__
B. Would you please come to my office immediately__

39

Circle the letter of the response below which tells why the following statement is <u>not</u> a polite request:

May I take this opportunity to thank you for your unselfish efforts in this year's United Way campaign___

A. The statement is <u>not</u> in question form.
B. The statement does <u>not</u> request any specific action.
C. The statement does <u>not</u> allow an option for refusal.
D. The statement is an indirect question.

40

Circle the letter of the statement below which indicates why the following question could be punctuated with a question mark rather than a period:

Would you please search your files and send me any information you have concerning local certified investment counselors?

A. The statement seeks no action.
B. The statement is a command.
C. The statement allows the person the option to refuse.
D. The statement is an imperative sentence.

41

Fill in the blanks below:

A. A polite request is stated in _____ form and is punctuated with a _____.
B. A polite request in the form of a command gives the person no option to _____ and is punctuated with a _____.
C. A polite request calls for a specific _____ rather than a(n) _____ to the question.

42

Read the following statement; then answer each of the four questions that follow with a simple yes or no:

Will you please review the enclosed document and send us your reaction by early spring.

A. Does the above statement seek action? _____
B. Does it expect a direct yes-or-no answer? _____
C. Does the period at the end imply an option to refuse? _____
D. Is the statement a polite request? _____

Read the following sentence; then circle the letter of the response which describes the sentence:

We have written to you several times in the past year asking if you will please come to our shop any day from 9 a.m. to 5 p.m. Monday through Friday___

A. a direct question
B. an indirect question
C. a polite request
D. a command

The sentence should be punctuated with _____ at the end.

▶ 43

Fill in the blanks below:

The requirements of a polite request are that the statement indeed be a _____ and the request be stated in _____ form. The request will call for _____ rather than words and will not require a direct _____.

▶ 44

Fill in the blanks with one of these phrases: a question mark, a period, or an exclamation point:

A direct question requires _____.
An emphatic statement of emotion takes _____.
An indirect question is normally punctuated by _____.
An interjection requires _____.

▶ 45

Fill in the blanks below with either period or question mark:

A simple polite request is punctuated with _____.
A request in the form of a command that allows the option to refuse is punctuated with _____.
A request in the form of a command that allows no choice except to act is punctuated with _____.

▶ 46

Make the necessary changes, deletions, and insertions in punctuation in these sentences:

A. Bravo. Mario's performance was the best ever, don't you agree.
B. To calculate m p g, simply divide _____ (two hundred five decimal point five) miles driven by _____ (eight decimal point two), the number of gallons used, to get _____ (twenty-five decimal point zero six) m.p.g..

▶ 47

Make the necessary changes, deletions, and insertions of punctuation in these sentences:

48

A. Would you please mail three checks by UPS for $18.00, $28, and $34. right away?

B. Mr C B Kepke resides at 113 S Cielo Ln in St Louis, MO. 63109-0443!

C. Aren't the F.D.A., F.H.A., U.S.O.E., and U.S.D.A. all departments within our U S Government.

You have just completed the first section of this program. Please read the directions for taking the section test. Keep in mind that in this first test your concern will be with periods, exclamation points, and question marks. Disregard commas for now.

▶▶ DIRECTIONS FOR THE SECTION TESTS*

1. Punctuate the communication which follows. Any punctuation that has not yet been presented in this text has been inserted for you.

2. Please note that this end-of-section test is not good business writing. Everything is extremely contrived and overpunctuated. The purpose is to cause you to over-learn. If you can punctuate the section tests, you should have no trouble with the final exam.

3. Carefully read the communication and insert punctuation as necessary. If you are handwriting, use a pencil so that you can change marks easily. Some instructors might tell you to type the communication using various hardware and/or software.

4. The (E) in the copy stands for the end of a sentence. You are to insert the proper end punctuation at these points.

5. Proofread your letter when finished and insert additional punctuation if necessary until you feel certain all punctuation is correct.

6. After you have completely finished, tear out the test key, which gives the communication as it should be punctuated. Circle all punctuation marks in your own copy that differ from the key.

7. This step is very important! Once your errors have been circled, find the numbers you missed on the REVIEW SHEET and read the number of the frame where that particular rule is discussed in the textbook. Be sure to go back and look up the suggested frame for every item missed before you continue to the next section. In this way you will profit from your mistakes, and misunderstandings will be cleared up immediately. When you review, you may want to ask the teacher to explain any items that are still unclear to you. Your teacher will be glad to provide this remedial attention when you show a genuine interest in learning. Finally, write a practice sentence for each item that you missed. Be careful to use correct punctuation.

8. The instructor will help you determine whether you are ready to continue to the next section or whether you need to review any preceding material.

*NOTE: Follow these instructions for each of the section tests. These directions will not be repeated for each section.

September 27, 19___

Mr John L Tinnerello
2505 Shady Shores Rd
Cleveland, OH 44127-6646

Dear Mr Tinnerello

Subject: Terminal Marks of Punctuation—Review of Findings

Wow Sec 1 hasn't been too bad, has it(E) Read on(E) Can you see why some companies, such as T R W, A T & T, and E D S choose to write their names without periods after the abbreviations(E) Why does a declarative or imperative sentence which ends with an abbreviation not require two periods, while a question mark or an exclamation point does follow an abbrev and period(E)

Periods are used as decimal points with whole nos that contain a decimal fraction, but not with even amounts such as _____ (thirty-nine dollars)(E) Related mixed amounts within the same sentence or paragraph should be consistent; i e, _____ (thirty-six dollars), _____ (seventeen dollars and twenty-seven cents), and _____ (forty dollars)(E)

An indirect question sounds and looks like a question but actually is a simple declarative sentence(E) Such statements require a period, not a question mark(E) What other kind of statement in question form uses a period(E) Right(E) Polite requests seek action rather than an answer to the question, don't they(E) Polite requests are actually subtle commands(E) If an option to refuse is intended, what mark of punctuation will be used(E) Right again(E) A question mark is used(E)

Obviously you are off to a great start(E) Keep up the fabulous work(E) Now, would you please turn to p. 19 and continue working this punctuation program(E)

Sincerely

Mrs Willene Whissenhunt
Dept of Communications and Public Relations

*NOTE: Ordinary words such as <u>Section</u> and <u>abbreviation</u> in Paragraph 1, <u>numbers</u> in Paragraph 2, and <u>page</u> in Paragraph 4 should not be abbreviated in ordinary written prose. They have been abbreviated here only to provide the necessary practice in punctuating abbreviations.

September 27, 19__

Mr.[1] John L.[2] Tinnerello
2505 Shady Shores Rd.[3]
Cleveland, OH[4] 44127-6646

Dear Mr.[5] Tinnerello

Subject: Terminal Marks of Punctuation — Review of Findings

Wow![6] Sec.[7] 1 hasn't been too bad, has it?[8] Read on.[9] Can you see why some companies, such as TRW,[10] AT&T,[11] and EDS[12] choose to write their names without periods after the abbreviations?[13] Why does a declarative or imperative sentence which ends with an abbreviation not require two periods, while a question mark or an exclamation point does follow an abbrev.[14] and period?[15]

Periods are used as decimal points with whole nos.[16] that contain a decimal fraction, but not with even amounts such as $39.[17] Related mixed amounts within the same sentence or paragraph should be consistent; i.[18] e.,[19] $36.00,[20] $17.[21] 27, and $40.[22] 00.[23]

An indirect question sounds and looks like a question but actually is a simple declarative sentence.[24] Such statements require a period, not a question mark.[25] What other kind of statement in question form uses a period?[26] Right![27] Polite requests seek action rather than an answer to the question, don't they?[28] Polite requests are actually subtle commands.[29] If an option to refuse is intended, what mark of punctuation will be used?[30] Right again![31] A question mark is used.[32]

Obviously you are off to a great start.[33] Keep up the fabulous work![34] Now, would you please turn to p.[35] 19 and continue working this punctuation program.[36]

Sincerely

Mrs.[37] Willene Whissenhunt
Dept.[38] of Communications and Public Relations

REVIEW SHEET

If you missed Number	See Frame Number	Practice Sentence
1	15	_____
2	15	_____
3	15	_____
4	21	_____
5	15	_____
6	7	_____
7	15	_____
8	10	_____
9	2, 3	_____
10	20, 17	_____
11	20, 17	_____
12	20, 17	_____
13	10	_____
14	19	_____
15	10, 19	_____
16	15, 16	_____
17	27	_____
18	15	_____
19	15, 16	_____
20	29	_____
21	25	_____
22	29	_____
23	2, 3	_____
24	2, 3	_____
25	2, 3	_____
26	10	_____
27	7	_____
28	10	_____
29	2, 3	_____
30	10	_____
31	7	_____

If you missed Number	See Frame Number	Practice Sentence
32	2, 3	_____
33	2, 3, 9*	_____
34	6	_____
35	15	_____
36	37, 38	_____
37	15	_____
38	15	_____

*See Feedback frame.

1

B. (The verb is missing in A; C is a phrase which contains neither a subject nor a verb.)

2

fact
command

3

A.
B.
C. (*You* is the understood subject of this imperative sentence.)

4

A. Friday. (*You* is the understood subject of this imperative sentence.)
B. (GNP). (This group of words is a complete sentence because it contains both a subject and a verb. Can you identify them?)

5

A. No punctuation (This is a dependent clause, which you will learn about in Section 3.)
B. businesses. (*Most* is the subject; *are* is the verb.)
C. No period should be placed at the end of this group of words.
D. insurance. (The requirements of a sentence have been met: *Anyone* is the subject of the sentence; *should have* is the verb.)

Remember, two spaces follow a period at the end of a sentence.

FEEDBACK

life!   (Strong emotion is apparent in these words.)

6

7

A. Great!   profits! or profits.
B. break!   wage!

An **interjection** is something that is thrown into a sentence without grammatical connection. The exclamation point indicates surprise, excitement, or strong feelings.

8

A. years!   (A startling fact is usually emphasized with an exclamation point.)
B. Terrific!   stocks!   (A period may be used at the end, depending upon the writer's intended emphasis.)

9

A. persistence.   (Probably a period is sufficient. Be careful not to overuse the exclamation point; use it for emphasis.)
B. No punctuation   (You are absolutely correct! This is not a complete sentence and should not be punctuated.)
C. widening. or !   (Only you, when you are writing a sentence, know what emphasis you want to convey.)

direct
indirect

10

B.

A.

A. produced?   (a direct question)
B. called.   (an indirect question) (In case you are interested, the difference between a country's exports and total imports is called its **balance of trade.**)

A. service.   (This statement is an indirect question; therefore, a question mark cannot be used.)
B. want?   (a direct question)
C. No punctuation   (This group of words does not form a complete sentence and therefore should not be punctuated.)

Medical Doctor   (No space follows the first abbreviation, but one space follows the completed abbreviation.)
Mister   (One space follows the complete abbreviation.)
Adler's middle name, which we have no way of knowing   (One space follows the initial.)
Senior   (One space follows the complete abbreviation.)
Miss   (*Miss* is not an abbreviation and therefore requires no period.)

16

A. a.m.↓
B. Ph.D.↓
C. i.e.,↓
D. Nos.↓

17

Ⓐ (YMCA with no periods is the common abbreviation.)

18

No   (The period after the abbreviation also serves as the period for the end of the sentence. *USSR* could also be written with no periods after the abbreviations. In this case, a period would be needed only to end the sentence.)

19

A. Wm.   Jr.   5:12 a.m.   (Only one period is used to end a sentence.)
B. Ms.   I.R.S.? or IRS?   (Ms. should be used before a woman's name unless her preferred title—Miss or Mrs.—is known.)

20

Yes (The University of California at Los Angeles writes UCLA with no periods.)

A. (COBOL)
(Stands for COmmon Business Oriented Language)
B. (No. 36)
(No. is the abbreviation for Number.)
C. (AFL-CIO)
(Stands for American Federation of Labor-Congress of Industrial Organizations)
D. (AAA)
(This well-known organization is almost always written without periods because that's the way the American Automobile Association writes its own name.)
E. (Phoenix, AZ 85068-1042)
(AZ stands for Arizona.) (Two-letter state abbreviations should be typed in capitals with no period or extra spacing following the last letter before the nine-digit ZIP Code. In case you are interested, ZIP stands for Zip Improvement Program.)

21

(C.) (Although B is usually true, C is the criterion of acceptability.)

22

A. U.S.   Mr. C. N. Velez.
B. S.   Dr. G. O. Valdez, Sr.?   (Did you remember that *Miss* is not an abbreviation?)

23

A. What!   Chas. E. Spiner Corp.   Chicago! or Chicago?   (The word *What* is an interjection. AMEX is the abbreviation for the AMerican Stock EXchange. This statement can be punctuated as a strong emotional statement or as a direct question.)
B. Ling Bros., Inc.,   E. Hamilton Dr., Jackson, MS 39209-4777.   (Bros., of course, is an abbreviation for Brothers. Only in a company name would this abbreviation be acceptable. When two-letter state abbreviations and ZIP Codes are used in addresses, no period follows the state abbreviation.)

24

decimal fraction
dollars from cents

25

A. .7   5.2
B. $42.75 $28.30

26

$35

27

A. $27.00   (This figure, $27, needs no decimal point and zeros because it is an even amount of money.)
B. This amount is correctly written.   (A period is used as a decimal point to separate dollars and cents in uneven amounts. Notice no spacing before or after the decimal point.)
C. $4.   (The even amount would require neither the zeros nor the decimal point.)
D. The amount is correctly written.   (The period is needed to end the sentence.)

28

Ⓐ. (In the second sentence, because the decimal point and cents are expressed in the first figure, the decimal point and zeros—cents—would also be expressed in the second amount, $1.<u>00</u>, for consistency.)

29 ▶

A. The sentence is correct.   (The decimal point and zeros should be included in the $29.00—even amount—to be consistent with the .95—decimal point and cents—in the first amount.)
B. $16.<u>00</u> $590.<u>00</u>   (All of these numbers are even amounts, thus not requiring decimal points or zeros. The period is needed, of course, after $590 to end the sentence.)
C. All figures are correct as written.   (Because even and uneven amounts are mixed in the same sentence, the even amount—$1.00—should be written with the decimal point and zeros for consistency.)
D. $13.<u>00</u> $28,080.<u>00</u>   (Both figures are even amounts, thus requiring no decimal point or zeros in either.)

30 ▶

A. 0.<u>3</u>   0.<u>9</u>
B. 17.<u>75</u> yds.<u></u>   15.<u>98</u> m.<u></u>

31 ▶

Action

32 ▶

does not

33 ▶

34

Ⓐ (Sentence B is a direct question and requires a direct answer.)

35

Ⓒ

36

question
does
question mark
NOTE: This statement does not ask for a specific action, but requires an answer instead.

37

No. 1   (The period indicates no option for refusal. The question mark allows a choice of either being quiet or not being quiet.)

38

Ⓑ Would you please come to my office immediately.   (Statement A could be either a polite request or a question, depending upon whether you intend to allow the option of refusal.)

B.

39

C.

40

A. question   period
B. refuse   period
C. action   answer

41

A. Yes
B. No
C. No
D. Yes

42

Ⓑ.
a period

43

44

request
question
action
answer

45

a question mark.
an exclamation point.
a period.
an exclamation point.

46

a period
a question mark
a period   (or an exclamation point, depending upon the emphasis needed)

47

A. Bravo /!   agree /?
B. m./p./g./,   205./5   8./2   25./06   m.p.g. /

A. $18 /00, $34 /   away ? .

B. Mr. C.B. Kepke   S. Cielo Ln.   St. Louis, MO / 63109-0443 ! .

C. F /D /A /, F /H /A /, U /S /O /E /, and U /S /D /A.   U.S. Government /?
(Should read: FDA, FHA, USOE, and USDA)

48

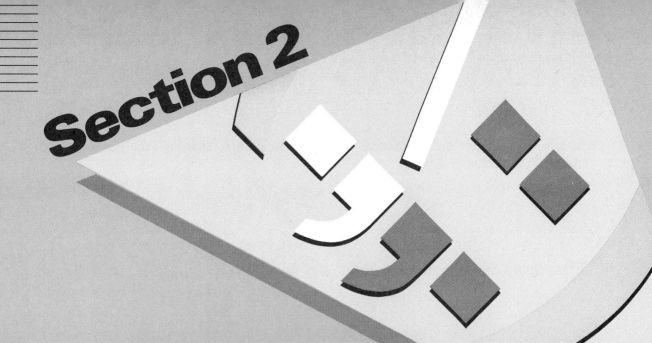

Section 2

Rule No. 6

A number containing more than four digits is difficult to read. Therefore, use a comma in numbers of four or more digits.

49

Wrong:	6873	47986	2073483
Right:	6,873	47,986	2,073,483

Is the following sentence punctuated correctly? _____

(Yes/No)

Over 20000 credit unions exist in the United States today.

50

Numbers are set off in groups of three. To punctuate figures of four or more digits, count three places left from the decimal point or from the far right digit of the whole number and insert a comma. Never insert commas in the decimal part of a number.

Insert a comma where appropriate in each of the following numbers:

588698 $39056   3921.7 $7702.15

51

Most numbers of _____ or more digits should be punctuated with a _____ so that they may be read easily.

52

Circle the numbers that should have commas and insert commas where appropriate:

532.6	48396	331	7687	$3972.23
81266	3.74326	$6978629	3819.47	392.6214

Of course, certain numbers should not be punctuated regardless of the number of digits they contain.

Ex.:	Year:	By the year 2000
	Address:	43472 W. Mulberry Street
	ZIP Code:	Atlanta, GA 30361-1327

53

Punctuate the following numbers correctly:

A. 807835 people
B. February 1977
C. 42736 Park Avenue

Other numbers that should not be punctuated are those that are meant to be read as one complete unit.

Ex.: 1. Loan #33829012
2. Credit Card Number 4275-0622-3752-1898
3. Social Security No. 852-02-6943

Would any of the long numbers below need commas? _____
(Yes/No)

54

If your answer is Yes, please insert commas where appropriate:

Account No. 48392018498
Check No. 2804
Room No. 8206
Telephone No. 213-472-8934
Page No. 3092

Punctuate the numbers in these sentences:

A. If total income is $26600 per year and taxes are $5300 per year, disposable income is $21300.
B. In 1987 there were about 5500 national banks and about 9000 state banks in the United States.
C. As a result, the owner responded to Proposition 927562 by lowering the price from $10652 to $9888.

55

Punctuate the numbers in these sentences:

A. The interest on an $85000 mortgage with a 12.0275 percent interest rate amounts to $10223.38 per year.
B. There are more than 3000 county governments and about 36000 city governments in this country.
C. In 1987 the total national debt was $2320.6 billion, which amounted to about $9400 per person.

56

Rule No. 7

Use commas to separate elements in a series. A **series** is <u>three</u> or more equally ranked elements (words, phrases, or clauses).

The sentence below contains a series of <u>words</u>. Underscore each element in the series.

The three roles that most people share are those of consumer, worker, and citizen.

57

58

On the lines below write the words that make up the series in the following sentence:

The business cycle may be defined as alternating periods of expansion and contraction in production, employment, income, and other economic activities.

_____   _____   _____   _____

59

No response is required for this frame. You will notice that this program prefers to put a comma before the conjunction which connects all the items in a series. If you learned that the comma before the <u>and</u>, <u>or</u>, and <u>nor</u> (conjunction) can be omitted, you may omit it. Both are considered correct by professional writers. However, the answers in this text will include the comma before the conjunction.

60

Punctuate the sentence below (at the points indicated) to separate the series of <u>phrases</u>:

Increased ease of expansion_ limited liability_ ease of transferring ownership_ and increased management skills are the four main advantages of a corporation.

61

The sentence below contains a series of <u>clauses</u> marked off by brackets. Punctuate this series of clauses:

If you have not already done so, someday you will conclude [that credit must be used prudently] [that it is a privilege] and [that it is an important asset].

62

Words that connect the elements of a series are called **conjunctions**. Conjunctions join together or connect two or more elements. In a series, conjunctions connect three or more elements.

    Ex.: 1. A consumer is a person or a business or a government that buys and uses goods or services.
        2. A consumer is a person, a business, or a government that buys and uses goods or services.

In the preceding examples, the comma replaces the conjunction _____ as the connector.

Each of the elements in the two sets of series below has been underlined.

> Credit is an agreement whereby a <u>government</u>, an <u>industry</u>, a <u>business</u>, or an <u>individual</u> may obtain the immediate use of <u>goods</u>, <u>services</u>, and <u>money</u> and pay for them at some future date.

The conjunction in the first series is _____.

The conjunction in the second series is _____.

63

A series must contain at least three elements. A sentence with only two elements contains a **binary** rather than a series. A binary (two parts) may also be connected by a conjunction.

> Ex.: **Series: Food, clothing, and shelter are basic economic needs.**
> **Binary: Food and shelter are basic economic needs.**

Why is the second example not a series? _____.

64

Circle the letter of the sentence below which contains a series:

A. Wealth consists of tangible goods that have monetary value because they are useful <u>and</u> desirable <u>and</u> relatively scarce.

B. Money is defined as anything that is generally accepted in exchange for goods <u>and</u> services <u>or</u> in payment of debts.

65

No comma is used after the connector in a series nor after the very last element in a series.

Mark these sentences RIGHT or WRONG:

1. _____ About 70 percent of all money transactions (payments for goods, services, and, debts) are made by check.

2. _____ A partnership is a business formed, owned, and managed, by two or more persons.

3. _____ Character, capacity, and capital are the "three Cs" of credit.

66

Which sentence below is punctuated correctly? _____
(A/B/Both/Neither)

A. Command, tradition, and, market are the three basic types of economies.

B. Raising large amounts of capital, having unlimited life, and being able to specialize more, are three major advantages of a corporation.

67

Carefully read the following sentence and fill in the blanks below:

Any government unit that issues a bond is required by law to make provision for paying the interest and to pay the debt when it becomes due.

68

In the above example, there are _____ requirements of the law: there-
(two/three)

fore, the sentence contains a _____. The connector is the word
(binary, series)

_____.

Underline the elements connected by the conjunction in each sentence below; then circle whether each sentence contains a binary or a series:

69

A. A term insurance policy is the simplest form of life insurance and provides a specified level of insurance for a fixed period of time. (Binary/Series)

B. Suppose that a husband and wife earn $60,000 each year, that there are four people in their family, and that each exemption results in a $3,000 decrease in the taxable income. (Binary/Series)

State whether each sentence below contains a binary, a series, neither, or both. Underscore each binary and circle the connector for every series.

A. The rates for services provided by public utilities, not government owned, are usually regulated by the state or the federal government.

70

_____
(Binary/Series/Neither/Both)

B. For example, suppose Mrs. Smith owns 100,000 shares of stock in an oil company in Oklahoma.

_____
(Binary/Series/Neither/Both)

State whether the two sentences below contain a binary, a series, neither, or both. Underscore each binary and circle the connector for every series.

A. The major phases of the business cycle are commonly called prosperity, crisis, recession, depression, and revival.

_____

(Binary/Series/Neither/Both)

B. The more than 250 million people in the United States want, need, and demand many economic goods and services.

_____

(Binary/Series/Neither/Both)

71

Remember, a series is punctuated with commas if all the connectors except the last one are missing. A binary (two elements) does not require the use of a comma.

Punctuate the sentences below, including the terminal marks of punctuation:

A. Comparison shopping means comparing the price of the product the quality of the product and the utility of the product to those of another brand
B. Every society faces the conflict between unlimited wants and limited resources
C. Every society has to develop an economic system to determine <u>what</u> type of goods should be produced <u>how much</u> of each <u>how</u> these goods should be produced and <u>for whom</u>

72

Sometimes a series ends with the word *etc.* to show that the series continues in thought. Although it should be avoided (the abbreviation tends to be overused), the word *etc.* should have commas around it — both <u>before</u> and <u>after</u> — when used.

Ex.: Such action would increase GNP, create jobs, reduce unemployment, <u>etc.</u>, according to most analysts.

The *etc.* indicates that there are several more elements in the series; therefore, a comma is placed both _____ and _____ the word *etc.*

73

Etc. stands for "and so forth." Never use the words *and etc.* together.

Ex.: The ability to make money, the expertise needed to manage it, the wisdom to spend it wisely, <u>and etc.</u>, are not necessarily found in the same individual.

Circle the letter below which identifies the meaning of *and etc.* as used in the example above:

A. and so forth
B. and and so forth

74

75

Is the sentence below stated correctly? _____
(Yes/No)

In a technological society special training, knowledge, skills, and etc. are usually rewarded by increased income.

76

Give two reasons why the preceding sentence is correct or incorrect.

1. _____

2. _____

77

When the conjunctions (connectors) are repeated, no commas are necessary since the commas usually take the place of the conjunctions. (See Frame 62.)

Circle the letter of each correctly punctuated sentence below:

A. The United States, and Russia, and Japan, and West Germany are the four leading industrial nations of the world.

B. In underdeveloped nations such as Nicaragua, Zaire, Pakistan, Sri Lanka, Kenya, etc. almost all of the personal income goes for food.

78

Circle the letter of each correctly punctuated sentence below:

A. Savings of individuals as well as families, savings of business firms, and extensions of bank credit, are a few general sources of loanable funds.

B. The board of directors decided that earnings would be used for further capital expansion, and that the next stock dividend would be double.

79

If you correctly answered every sentence in the last two frames, you are doing extremely well. Please continue.

Does the following sentence contain a series? _____
(Yes/No)

Each person's income depends on the quantity of resources which he or she contributes to production and, of course, on the price which these resources command in the market place.

Underline the two conjunctions in the sentence in the preceding frame and write what they connect.

▶ **80**

_____

_____

In punctuating a series, you may choose either to use or not to use a comma before the conjunction that introduces the last item. Both ways are considered correct. (See Frame 59.)

Right: onions, peas, and carrots
Right: onions, peas and carrots

Which of the following sentences is punctuated correctly? _____

▶ **81**

(A/B/Both/Neither)

A. As you have seen, our personal attitudes toward work, savings, and education can affect the country's productive ability.
B. Higher costs for labor, fertilizer, fuel and machines might combine to cause a reduction in the supply of corn.

Although the comma before the conjunction in a series is usually optional, many publishers, reporters, and business people prefer to use it for the simple reason that the omission of the comma is often confusing. Compare the following sentences:

A. To complete the transaction, you have to sell these items: livestock, equipment, buildings and land.
B. To complete the transaction, you have to sell these items: livestock, equipment, buildings, and land.

▶ **82**

In the above examples the intended meaning was to have buildings and land separate, making four items in the series. Which sentence better conveys this meaning? _____

(A/B)

Again, the comma before the conjunction may _not_ be optional, depending on the meaning. Observe the following sentence:

The carpeting was available in the following colors: gold, red, tan, aqua, dark brown, orange and black, blue, and green.

Circle the letter below which tells how many different rug colors are in the series above:

▶ **83**

A. 7
B. 8
C. 9

84 Punctuate the following sentence so that blue and green are the same rug, making only seven rug colors in the series:

The carpeting was available in the following colors: gold red tan aqua dark brown orange and black blue and green

85 Cross out or insert commas or words as needed to correct the punctuation in the following sentence:

A. New partners may contribute their personal skills, money, or, even ideas, to the business.
B. Electric, water, natural gas, telephone companies, and etc. are examples of monopolies in most communities.

86 Make the necessary corrections in punctuation in the following sentence:

More than half of those in the $10000–$20000 annual income bracket say they would feel secure with $50000 or less in savings, while half of those with annual incomes of more than $50000 say they would need at least $200000.

87 Circle the letter of each correctly punctuated sentence below:

A. The articles of incorporation give the name, and address, and type of business for the corporation.
B. The articles of incorporation give the name, address, and type of business for the corporation.
C. The articles of incorporation give the name and address and type of business for the corporation.

88 Punctuate these sentences:

A. This is especially true with respect to how each firm prices its product what services each firm offers and how much each produces.
B. Fire lightning theft window breakage upset etc will be covered under "comprehensive" insurance.

Add or delete punctuation to make these sentences correct:

A. Whole life, limited payment, endowment, and, term, are the four main types of life insurance policies.
B. Often a partnership is formed by one person who has the skill to run the business and another who has the money to get it started.

89 ▶

Rule No. 8

Use commas to set off the year when it follows the month and day, except a date that ends a sentence.

> Ex.: 1. **On November 4, 1992, the elections . . .**
> 2. **. . . by April 15, 1995.**

As shown in the above examples, when the date comes in the middle of the sentence, _____ are placed _____ and _____ the year.

90 ▶

A specific date usually consists of three parts—the month, the day, and the year (December 6, 1941). If the date is stated in only one or two parts, no commas are required.

> Ex.: 1. **In March the Senate voted . . .**
> 2. **The last prime rate increase on April 10 was the . . .**

How many parts do these dates contain?

Before September . . . _____
By February 3 . . . _____
On Thursday, April 24, the . . . _____
November 1988 _____
On July 23, 1893, the . . . _____

91 ▶

Although a date consisting of two units does not require a comma, some writers prefer commas around the year when it is preceded by the name of the month.

Right: She ran for vice president in November 1984 and lost.
Right: She ran for vice president in November, 1984, and lost.

Is the following sentence punctuated correctly? _____
(Yes/No)

Interest rates increased in January, 1985 and again in August, 1985.

92 ▶

93

Circle the letter of the correctly punctuated phrase below:

  A. Thanksgiving on November 26, will be . . .

  B. December 28, 1941, was the date . . .

94

Frequently a date will occur with a preposition at the beginning of a sentence. If the phrase is short and the date consists of only one or two parts, no comma is required.

  Ex.: **1. In July we took a complete inventory.**

       2. On July 31 the company plans to switch to CAR.

Where should commas be placed in this prepositional phrase?

By March 29 1937 the automobile had become a household word in the U.S.

95

Circle the letter of the correctly punctuated phrase below:

  A. During August, 1958 the United Nations . . .

  B. Our appointment is for Tuesday, October 19, at 2 p.m. in the . . .

96

Punctuate the following sentence if necessary:

In August 1997 our Milan facility will be ready for production.

97

If a date has three parts or more, commas are required between the parts and to set off the year.

  Ex.: On Monday, October 19, 1987, "Black Monday" occurred on Wall Street.

Punctuate the following sentence:

Adam Smith's *Wealth of Nations* was published on May 17, 1776 the year of the Declaration of Independence.

98

Circle the letter of each correctly punctuated sentence below:

  A. In July, 1867, the U.S. purchased Alaska from Russia.

  B. In July 1867, the U.S. purchased Alaska from Russia.

  C. In July 1867 the U.S. purchased Alaska from Russia.

  D. In July, 1867 the U.S. purchased Alaska from Russia.

Cross out any <u>unnecessary</u> commas in the following sentences:

A. June 14, 1991, July 12, 1992, August 7, 1993, and September 10, 1994, are the dates for the next four conventions.
B. Since April 6, the Federal Reserve has been increasing the money supply.
C. From Saturday, December 17, through Monday, December 26, all suburban stores will stay open until midnight.

99

The date at the top of a letter requires a comma only between the day and the year.

Ex.: January 25, 1999

The date at the beginning of a letter consists of _____ parts, but no comma follows the year in this case.

100

Punctuate the following sentences:

A. On June 25 1975 Mozambique gained its independence from Portugal.
B. In May 1945 the Netherlands was liberated from Germany.

101

Punctuate these two sentences:

A. The anniversary dinner will be held on Tuesday September 13 at 7:30 p.m.
B. In March 1818 Karl Marx was born; he published *Das Kapital* in September 1867 and *The Communist Manifesto* in 1848.

102

Rule No. 9

Use commas to set off the name of the state or country when the name of the city precedes it.

Ex.: 1. **Pikes Peak near Colorado Springs, Colorado, is one of the best-known mountains in the Rockies.**
2. **Istanbul, Turkey, was known as Constantinople in the 12 Century A.D.**

As shown in the above examples, _____ are placed both _____ and _____ the state or country following the name of a city.

103

104

Circle the letter of each correctly punctuated sentence below:

A. St. Louis, Missouri, is known as the "Gateway to the West."
B. The area around Harrodsburg, Kentucky was the first permanent settlement west of the Allegheny Mountains.

105

Students usually place a comma between the city and state, but rarely remember to put a comma after the state when it falls in the middle of a sentence.

What is wrong with the following sentence?

Founded in 1565, St. Augustine, Florida is the oldest permanent city in the continental United States.

106

Punctuate the following sentence:

San Antonio Texas and San Diego California are two of the earliest Spanish missions in this country.

107

Because the ZIP Code is considered the same unit as the name of the state, no comma should separate the state and the ZIP Code number.

Ex.: 1529 Medbury
Detroit, MI 48211-5565

How many units make up the last line in the above address? _____

108

Each of the following items is the last line of a letter address. Insert and delete commas as necessary to correctly punctuate each address.

A. Great Falls MT 59404-6934
B. Elizabethtown PA, 17022-4681
C. Charleston, SC, 29404-6915

The ZIP Code should be typed on the same line as the name of the state with only one or two spaces between the state and ZIP Code. Observe these addresses:

1. 4000 Linkwood Road   2. Silver Spring, MD 20902-5841
   Baltimore, MD 21210-2202

Should a comma be placed after MD in the above examples: _____
                                                     (Yes/No)

Should a comma be placed in the ZIP Code, which is a nine-digit number?

_____
(Yes/No)

109

In addressing mail in the 1990s, leave one or two spaces between the state abbreviation and the ZIP Code—preferably <u>one</u> space as shown throughout this text.

Circle the letter of each correctly written address below:

A. Montepelier, VT   05602-7974
B. Camden, AR 71701-9431
C. Monroe L.A. 71201-5890

110

Delete the unnecessary commas in the following sentences:

A. Butte, Montana, and Cheyenne, Wyoming, are competing cities for airline service.
B. New York, Los Angeles, Chicago, Houston, and, Philadelphia, are the top five U.S. cities according to the Census Bureau, on Friday, October, 16.

111

Add commas as needed to correctly punctuate these sentences:

A. American Airlines has nonstop flights daily to such destinations as Tokyo Japan Paris France Brussels Belgium Cophenhagen Denmark and Athens Greece.
B. The convention will begin in Salt Lake City Utah on August 20 1997 and will conclude on August 28.

112

Watch for review items as you punctuate the following sentences:

A. The map "Mount St Helens and vicinity March 1981" may be purchased for $220 (two dollars and twenty cents) from the Federal Center in Denver Colorado if you order before 5 p m, June 30
B. In 1665 the Great Plague killed 75000 people in London England and 58000 people in Dublin Ireland

113

114

Watch for review again as you punctuate these sentences:

A. On August 10 1839 the family of Simone W Carson Jr moved to 9914 Lakewood Avenue Cleveland Ohio and started a chain of dry-cleaning stores

B. Gandhi was assassinated on January 30 1948 in New Delhi India by a Hindu fanatic

115

Rule No. 10

If you are writing to a specific person at a company, you should include that person's title in the inside address.

Ex.: **Mr. Wayne R. Hoffman, President**
Hoffman, Hoffman & Associates
7915 Moseley Blvd.
Fort Wayne, IN 46807-0309

Circle Mr. Hoffman's position title in the above address.

You will also notice that in the address lines every individual's full name is preceded by an informal title.

Ex.: <u>Mr.</u> **Wayne R. Hoffman, President**

116

A comma _____ separate the last name from the position title
             (does/does not)

in an address. A comma _____ separate the title and the person's
             (does/does not)

first name.

Observe the following address again:

Mr. Wayne R. Hoffman, President
Hoffman, Hoffman & Associates
7915 Mosley Blvd.
Fort Wayne, IN 46807-0309

Notice that there is <u>no</u> punctuation after each line of the address unless it ends with an abbreviation. The outdated practice of placing a comma after each line and a period at the end of an address has long been discarded by modern business writers. Also, do not use a comma before an ampersand (&) in a company name unless you know that a particular company prefers to do so.

Punctuate the following address lines of a business letter:

Ms Gloria Alvarez Office Manager
Adams-Smith Company
58342 McCrary Pl
Brighton
ENGLAND

117

Each of the following is the first line of an address. Circle the letter of each correct line:

A. Reverend, James R. Petersen, Treasurer
B. Mrs. Pat Scriabin Marketing Manager
C. Professor Wm. C. Scott, Head

118

Use commas to set off titles and degrees which directly follow a person's name.

Ex.: 1. Miss Cecelia Williams, public relations consultant, joined the firm in May.

As shown above, _____ should be placed (before/after/before and after) a person's title in a sentence.

119

Punctuate the sentence and the address below:

A. Mrs. Carolyn Gentry receptionist asked me . . . (sentence)
B. Dr. Suzanne LaBrecque Dean (address)

120

Should a comma be placed <u>after</u> the person's title in a sentence? _____
Should a comma be placed <u>after</u> the person's title in an address? _____

121

122

Punctuate the following sentence:

The award went to Ernestine Lightfoot placement coordinator for her outstanding service.

123

What is wrong with the punctuation in the following sentence?

Brooke Yoder was named, assistant to the president, by the Board of Governors.

124

Delete and add commas as necessary in the following sentences:

A. Dr. Elaine M. Guthrie, vice president, of public relations presented a research paper in Singapore.

B. We need a new, systems analyst, for the newly opened Asian Pacific office.

125

Commas are also used around abbreviated titles like Jr., Sr., M.D., Ph.D., etc., when they <u>follow</u> a person's name.

NOTE: Some authorities contend that separating the titles <u>Jr.</u> and <u>Sr.</u> is not necessary anymore. However, such titles <u>are</u> usually separated when used in an address or when the individual prefers that the comma be used in his name. Rather than make you guess how to treat this inconsistency (preference), this program asks that you treat all titles the same: Punctuate them with a comma.

Address: Mr. James C. Cole, Sr.

Sentence: Dr. Amie S. Consuella, M.D., accepted a position at St. Luke's Hospital in Boston, Massachusetts.

As shown above, commas are placed around an abbreviated _____ in a sentence and _____ the name and abbreviated title in an address.

126

Is the following name punctuated correctly? _____
(Yes/No)

Mr. C. Blain Hoskinson Jr.

127

Watch for review items as you add the necessary punctuation to these sentences:

A. Francis R Kendall MD of Tulsa Oklahoma was named president of the O E O

B. On April 15 1979 Jimmy Carter President of the U S called on all citizens to drive 15 miles less per week, which would result in a savings of about 450000 barrels of oil per day

Watch for review again as you insert and delete punctuation for the following items:

A. Mrs Louise J Hampton, D.D.S. of Cherryville, Pennsylvania was elected president, of the A.D.A.

B. Miss Kayla Rivera MD
19826 Krenshaw Ave
Springlake, N.J., 07762-4700

128 ▶

Rule No. 11

Use commas to set off the abbreviations *Inc.* and *Ltd.* when they directly follow the company name.

NOTE: Again, some people prefer to omit the comma here claiming that the "newer style" makes such punctuation unnecessary. Indeed, many business newspapers and journals frequently omit a comma before the words *Inc.* and *Ltd.* However, many writers still include it. Again, it's mostly a matter of personal preference. This program will use a comma before the words *Inc.* and *Ltd.* and asks that you do the same while working with this text.

129 ▶

> **Ex.: Texas Instruments, Inc.**
> **Bateman, James & Klausmeier, Ltd.**

Punctuate the following first lines of company addresses:

A. Baldwin and Willis Ltd.

B. Davis, Decker, and Devereaux Inc.

Correct the punctuation of the following lines:

A. Watkins and Meyers, Ltd of Liverpool England . . .

B. Munton, Young, and Ashley Inc. since 1974 . . .

130 ▶

Punctuate the following items:

A. Grace Sheek & Sons Ltd (company address; Grace Sheek is the principal stockholder.)

B. Deaver Hibler and Stevens Inc and DeWeese-McFaddin Ltd (two corporations)

131 ▶

132

Although commas are placed around *Inc.* and *Ltd.*, no commas are necessary to set off the words *Company* or *Corporation* when they follow a company name.

Ex.: 1. **Bercor Corporation is listed by NASDAQ.**
 2. **The I. C. Rhodes Company**

Cross out incorrect punctuation in the following sentence:

The Justine, Corporation, merged with the Uston, Company to become Just-Us, Inc., in 1989.

133

Circle the letter of the correctly punctuated phrase below:

A. The Quik-Sale, Corporation presented a proposal to . . .
B. A rate increase for New Mexico Power and Light, Company, went into effect . . .
C. Jamboree, Inc., bought the . . .
D. Everyone supported Krepps, Collier & Baggett, Ltd. until they . . .

134

Punctuate the sentence below:

Emma Moon PhD Juanita Kliendienst M A Joe Lynch D D S and Harold Skaggs Jr flew to Auckland New Zealand Brisbane Australia and Jakarta Indonesia on Tuesday June 20

135

Research has shown that about 75 percent of all punctuation errors are in the misuse of the comma. Insert and delete <u>commas</u> as needed in the following sentence:

The following companies hired new resource personnel for the, 1990, expansion program: Pierpoint Industries Inc. added Gladys Brown contracts administrator; the Holly, Corporation of Birmingham, Alabama employed Richard Wade Jr. administrative assistant formerly of the General Electric, Company; and Adams, and Adams, Ltd. hired Percey Lipton Sr and Glenda Symington, as, electrical engineers.

136

Rule No. 12

Use a comma following the complimentary close of a letter in mixed punctuation style.

Ex.: Sincerely yours,

The complimentary close occurs at the (beginning/middle/end) of a letter.

Write the most common, although not necessarily the most frequently used, complimentary close that starts with a *Y* and punctuate it.

Y _____

137

In the signature lines, which come after the complimentary close, a comma will separate the writer's typed name and title when placed on the same line. No comma will follow the name if the title is placed on a separate line.

Right: Very truly yours,   Wrong: Cordially yours,

Vic Seeger, Director   Mrs. Sally Wiedeman,
                                     State Consultant

Why is the above example on the right incorrect? _____

_____

138

Circle the letters of the signature lines below which are punctuated correctly:

A. Dr. Carrie Ausbrooks,
   President-elect
B. Paul Gibson, Jr.,
   Director of Public Relations
C. James Vaughan
   Certified Public Accountant

139

Rule No. 13

If a comma is used following the complimentary close, a colon must be used after the salutation, which starts out the letter. The colon and comma used together after these letter parts is known as **mixed** punctuation.

Punctuate the following as <u>mixed</u> punctuation:

Dear Miss Jodzko

   D.S.

— — — — — — — — — —
— — — — — — — — — —
— — — — — — — — — —
— — — — — — — — — —

      D.S.
     Yours sincerely

140

141

The **open** punctuation style, which requires no punctuation at all after the salutation or complimentary close, is an alternative to mixed punctuation. Either mixed (using the colon and comma) or open (using no punctuation) is acceptable. Unless told otherwise, please used <u>mixed</u> punctuation for your responses in this text.

Compare: A. Dear Mr. Podorsky<u>:</u> . . . Very truly yours<u>,</u>
B. Ladies and Gentlemen_ . . . Yours sincerely_

Which one of the above is correct? _____
(A/B/Both)

142

In personal business letters, using the person's first name in the salutation is acceptable. In this case either a comma or a colon may be used.

Punctuate the following salutation:

Dear Dolly_

143

A colon is <u>always</u> acceptable after a salutation unless <u>open</u> punctuation has been stipulated; a comma may be used in a personal business letter when the first name is used; a semicolon is <u>never</u> appropriate.

Punctuate the following salutation:

Dear Mr. Blackstone_

144

Is the comma correct punctuation after this salutation?

Ladies and Gentlemen, _____
(Yes/No)

145

On the line directly following each of the salutations below, write whether the punctuation following the salutation is correct or incorrect.

Dear Ms. Perez,   _____
Dear Joe,   _____
Dear Hank: _____
Dear Sirs and Madams;   _____

Circle A or B in each set below to indicate the correct item in each pair:

A. Dear Dr. Hammer: A. Dear Mr. Zapata,   A. Dear Michael:

B. Dear Muhammad;   B. Dear Cory,   B. Dear Janet,

146

If you were directed to use open punctuation, how would you punctuate the following salutation?

Dear Mr. and Mrs. Vanderstraaten_

147

The punctuation style you have been asked to use in punctuating the materials in this instructional program is called (mixed/open) punctuation and requires (a colon/no colon) after the _____ and (a comma/no comma) after the _____.

148

Punctuate these letter parts:

Dear Ms Wilson

— — — — — — — — — —

        Sincerely yours

149

This is the end of Section 2. Take the section test for Section 2. Follow the same directions given before the Section 1 test. After you have inserted all marks of punctuation, turn the page and check yourself. The final page is for your review; it lists all the items in the test by number and tells you in what frame you can review the item. Be sure to go back and look up any items you missed before continuing to Section 3. The information in Section 2 serves as a foundation for the materials that are to come in the remaining sections.

October 10 19___

Ms Lou Woods PhD
1612 Highland Ave
Bridgeport CT 06604-9927

Dear Ms Woods

In 1989 Thompson Ramo and Wooldridge Inc undertook a study from January 1 1980 through December 31 1988 which was just completed in May 1989(E) We wanted to know if Minneapolis Minnesota or Indianapolis Indiana would be suitable for a relocation and if Claude W Cheek Jr first vice president could lead TRW back to its position of prominence with NASA(E)

The results of this research and the company interest that it generated sent waves of excitement through our Accounting Marketing and Personnel Departments(E) Ms Vivian Samuelson chairman of the board wrote the Evans Long & Aston Corporation on Tuesday May 23 and told them of our intent to make a decision before December 1989(E) She stressed that although the cost of $175000 (one hundred seventy-five thousand dollars) for the study and $3850000 (three million eight hundred fifty thousand dollars) for the company move might seem extravagant and that stability status and growth were not guaranteed, she was intrigued by the possibilities(E)

What is your reaction to the attached report(E) Are the conclusions reasonable(E) Should Detroit Michigan Des Moines Iowa Topeka Kansas etc have been included(E)

Mr Richard Hunter Miss Rebecca Reiter Mrs Jean Phillips and Mr John R Day Sr will all be in Hartford Connecticut on Saturday November 14(E) Could you meet with them sometime during that morning go over the report with them and tell them your initial reactions(E) If not, I wonder if you would mind telephoning me right away(E)

TRW sincerely appreciates the time energy and money you have spent on this project(E) Won't you let me hear from you soon(E)

Sincerely yours

Terry O McLane Director
Marketing Operations

omb

Attachment

BUSINESS LETTER

October 10,[1] 19___

Ms.[2] Lou Woods,[3] Ph.[4]D.[5]
1612 Highland Ave.[6]
Bridgeport, CT[7] [8] 06604-9927

Dear Ms.[9] Woods:[10]

In 1989[11] Thompson,[12] Ramo,[13] and Wooldridge,[14] Inc.,[1516] undertook a study from January[17] 1,[18] 1980,[19] through December 31,[20] 1988,[21] which was just completed in May[22] 1989.[23] We wanted to know if Minneapolis,[24] Minnesota, or Indianapolis,[25] Indiana,[26] would be suitable for a relocation[27] and if Claude W.[28] Cheek,[29] Jr.,[3031] first[32] vice president,[33] could lead TRW[34] back to its position of prominence with NASA.[35]

The results of this research[36] and the company interest that it generated sent waves of excitement through our Accounting,[37] Marketing,[38] and Personnel Departments.[39] Ms.[40] Vivian Samuelson,[41] chairman of the board,[42] wrote the Evans, Long[43] &[44] Aston[45] Corporation[46] on Tuesday,[47] May 23,[48] and told them of our intent to make a decision before December[49] 1989.[50] She stressed that although the cost of $175,[51]000 for the study and $3,850,000[52] for the company move might seem extravagant[53] and that stability,[54] status,[55] and growth were not guaranteed, she was intrigued by the possibilities.[56]

What is your reaction to the attached report?[57] Are the conclusions reasonable?[58] Should Detroit,[59] Michigan,[60] Des Moines,[61] Iowa,[62] Topeka,[63] Kansas,[64] etc.,[6566] have been included?[67]

Mr.[68] Richard Hunter,[69] Miss[70] Rebecca Reiter,[71] Mrs.[72] Jean Phillips,[73] and Mr.[74] John R.[75] Day,[76] Sr.,[7778] will all be in Hartford,[79] Connecticut, on Saturday,[80] November 14.[81] Could you meet with them sometime during that morning,[82] go over the report with them,[83] and tell them your initial reactions?[84] If not, I wonder if you would mind telephoning me right away.[85][86]

TRW[87] sincerely appreciates the time,[88] energy,[89] and money you have spent on this project.[90] Won't you let me hear from you soon.[91]

Sincerely yours,[92]

Terry O.[93] McLane,[94] Director
Marketing Operations

omb

Attachment

REVIEW SHEET

If you missed Number	See Frame Number	Practice Sentence
1	100	
2	15	
3	119	
4	15, 16	
5	15, 16	
6	15	
7	103	
8	107, 109	
9	15	
10	140, 141	
11	94	
12	57	
13	59	
14	129	
15	15	
16	130	
17	90, 97	
18	97	
19	90, 97	
20	97	
21	92	
22	2	
23	103	
24	103–105	
25	103	
26	103–105	
27	64	
28	15	
29	125	
30	15	
31	125	

If you missed Number	See Frame Number	Practice Sentence
32	119, 121	
33	20	
34	20, 22	
35	2	
36	64, 68	
37	57	
38	59	
39	2	
40	15	
41	119	
42	119, 121	
43	57	
44	117	
45	132	
46	132	
47	91, 97	
48	97	
49	91, 92	
50	2	
51	49–51	
52	27	
53	64, 68	
54	57	
55	59	
56	2	
57	10	
58	10	
59	103	
60	103–105	
61	103	
62	103, 104, 57	
63	103	
64	103, 104, 73	
65	15	

If you missed Number	See Frame Number	Practice Sentence
66	73	_____
67	10	_____
68	15	_____
69	57	_____
70	15	_____
71	57	_____
72	15	_____
73	59	_____
74	15	_____
75	15	_____
76	125	_____
77	15	_____
78	125	_____
79	103	_____
80	103–105	_____
81	97	_____
82	2	_____
83	57	_____
84	59	_____
85	10	_____
86	10, 11	_____
87	20	_____
88	57	_____
89	59	_____
90	2	_____
91	33, 35	_____
92	136, 141	_____
93	15	_____
94	119, 120	_____

No (The figure should be written 20,000.)

49

588,698 $39,056   3,921.7 $7,702.15

50

four
comma

51

532.6   (48,396)   331   (7,687) $3,972.23
(81,266)   3.74326   ($6,978,629) (3,819.47)   392.6214

52

A. 807,835
B. No punctuation necessary
C. No punctuation necessary

53

63

No   (Usually only amounts and quantities require commas.)

54

55

A. $26,600 $5,300 $21,300
B. 5,500   9,000
C. $10,652 $9,888

56

A. $85,000 $10,223.38
B. $3,000   36,000
C. $2,320.6 billion $9,400   (Exceedingly large amounts are frequently stated this way to avoid confusion in reading the figure.)

57

consumer   worker   citizen

production   employment   income   other economic activities

58

No response is required for this frame.

59

Increased ease of expansion, limited liability, ease of transferring ownership, and increased management skills . . .

60

prudently,   privilege,

61

or

62

63

or
and

64

The example does <u>not</u> contain at least three elements.

65

(A) (Sentence B contains two binaries: (1) goods <u>and</u> services and (2) in exchange for goods and services <u>or</u> in payment of debts. In Sentence A the connector word *and* has been used rather than a comma.)

66

1. WRONG
2. WRONG
3. RIGHT

67

Neither   (In Sentence A, no comma should follow the conjunction in a series. In Sentence B, no comma should follow the last element in a series.)

two   (The two legal requirements are to make provision to pay the interest and to pay the debt when it becomes due.)

binary   (bi means two)

and

NOTE: As you can see, one must sometimes read carefully to determine the meaning.

68 ▶

A. A term insurance policy is the simplest form of life insurance and provides a specified level of insurance for a fixed period of time.
   (Binary)

B. Suppose that a husband and wife earn $60,000 each year, that there are four people in their family, and that each exemption results in a $3,000 decrease in the taxable income.
   (Series)

69 ▶

A. Binary   (the state or the federal government)

B. Neither

   Since neither contained a series, no connectors would be circled.

70 ▶

A. Series   (This series, containing five elements, has the word (and) as the connector.)
B. Both   (The series is want, need, (and) demand. The binary is <u>goods</u> and <u>services</u>.)

71

A. the price of the product, the quality of the product,   brand.
B. resources.   (The conjunction connects the binary <u>unlimited wants</u> and <u>limited resources</u>.)
C. produced,   each,   produced,   whom.

72

before and after

73

B. (Can you see that putting *and* before *etc.* creates "<u>and</u> <u>and</u> so forth," which is redundant?)

74

No

75 ▶

Reason #1: The word *and* and the abbreviation *etc.* should never be written together.
Reason #2: *etc.*, when used, should have a comma <u>after</u> it as well as before it.

76 ▶

Neither sentence is correct.   (In Sentence A either the *ands* or the *commas* should be omitted—one connector is sufficient. In Sentence B the *etc.* should have a comma following it as well as preceding it.)

77 ▶

Neither sentence is correct.   (In Sentence A no comma should follow the last item in a series. In Sentence B the conjunction connects the binary <u>that earnings would be</u> . . . and <u>that the next stock dividend</u> . . . , so no comma should precede the conjunction.)
NOTE: Three consecutive periods with one space before and after each period as used in this feedback frame form an **ellipsis**. An **ellipsis** is used to show that one or more words in a sentence have been omitted.

78 ▶

No   (The sentence contains a binary. *Of course* is a parenthetical expression, which will be covered later in this text.)

79 ▶

80

<u>or</u>   he . . . she
<u>and</u>   on the quantity of resources . . . on the price which these resources . . .
The ellipsis has been used again to indicate that words have been omitted.

81

Both   (The comma may be used before the conjunction and the last item in a series, or the comma may be omitted before the conjunction and the last item.)

82

B.

83

Ⓑ

. . . gold, red, tan, aqua, dark brown, orange and black, <u>blue and green</u>. (Do you see how the use of one comma can change the meaning of a sentence?)

84 ▶

A. or,   ideas,
B. and   etc.,

85 ▶

$10,000–$20,000 . . . $50,000 or less . . . $50,000 say . . . $200,000.   (There is no series in this sentence. Only the amounts of money—all over four digits—require commas.)

86 ▶

B. and C.

87 ▶

A. product,   offers,
B. Fire, lightning, theft, window breakage, upset, etc.,

88 ▶

71

89

A. and/,   term/,
B. The sentence is correct.   (This sentence contains a binary rather than a series.)

90

commas
before and after

91

one (month)
two (month and day)
three (day of week, month, and date)
two (month and year)
three (month, day, and year)

92

No   (If commas are used with the month and year, a comma is placed <u>after</u> the year as well as before. You know by now, don't you, that a comma should never precede a period at the end of a sentence?)

(B.)

93

March 29, 1937,   (Do you see that this is a three-part date and requires commas around the year regardless of the short prepositional phrase?)

94

(B.)   (In Sentence A *if* you choose to use commas, one will also be placed *after* the year.)

95

The sentence is correct as is.   (The prepositional phrase at the beginning is short, so no comma is required after 1997. August, 1997, is also correct since some writers prefer to set off the year when it is preceded by the name of the month.)

96

May 17, 1776,

97

(A.) and (C.)   (A—Some writers choose to place commas around the year preceded by the month. B—If no comma is used after July, no comma is necessary after 1867 because the prepositional phrase is short. C—This is the way month and year are usually written because it is only a two-part date. D—If a comma is used after July, a comma is necessary after 1867.)

98

A. All commas are necessary; all are three-part dates.
B. Since April 6⁄ (This is a short introductory prepositional phrase.)
C. All commas are necessary; all are three-part dates.

99

three

100

A. June 25, 1975,
B. No punctuation is required. (Commas around , 1945, would be acceptable.)

101

A. Tuesday, September 13,
B. No punctuation is required. (Commas around , 1818, and , 1867, are optional.)

102

commas
before and after

103

Ⓐ (Sentence B should have a comma after Kentucky as well as before Kentucky.)

104 ▶

There should be a comma after Florida. (A comma is placed <u>after</u> the state as well as between the city and state.)

105 ▶

San Antonio, Texas, and San Diego, California, (Did you remember to put commas both before and after the state?)

106 ▶

---

two (The city is one; the state and ZIP Code together form the second unit.)

107 ▶

A. Great Falls, MT 59404-6934
B. Elizabethtown, PA / 17022-4681
C. Charleston, SC / 29404-6915

108 ▶

No

No   (A ZIP Code is considered a number of a serial nature.)

109

Ⓑ (In Example A too much space separates the state abbreviation and the ZIP Code. In Example C a comma should separate the city and state, and the two-letter state abbreviation should contain no periods.)

110

A. This sentence is correct.   (Commas surround the state when preceded by the name of the city.)

B. and/, Philadelphia/,   Bureau/,   October/,

111

A. Tokyo, Japan, Paris, France, Brussels, Belgium, Copenhagen, Denmark, Athens,

B. Salt Lake City, Utah,   August 20, 1997,

NOTE: Semicolons could be used after each country for better clarity.

112

A. St. Helens $2.20   Denver, Colorado,   5 p.m.   June 30.

B. 75,000   London, England,   58,000   Dublin, Ireland.

113

A. August 10, 1839,   Simone W. Carson, Jr.,   Avenue,   Cleveland, Ohio,   stores.
B. January 30, 1948,   New Delhi, India,   fanatic.

114

President

115

does
does not

116

Ms. Gloria Alvarez, Office Manager
Adams-Smith Company
58342 McCrary Pl.
Brighton
ENGLAND

117

118
C. (In Sentence A no comma should separate a title and an individual's first name. In Sentence B a comma should separate a person's last name and the following position title.)

119
commas
before and after

120
A. Gentry, receptionist,
B. LaBrecque, Dean   (Of course a title that <u>precedes</u> a person's name is not set off with commas.)

121
Yes   (unless the title is the end of the sentence)
No   (If you said yes, reread Instructional Frames 115 and 117.)

Ernestine Lightfoot, placement coordinator,

122 ▶

The title <u>assistant to the president</u> does not directly follow the person's name; therefore, commas should not be used.

123 ▶

A. vice president / of public relations,
B. new / systems analyst /

124 ▶

title
between

125 ▶

No   (A comma should separate Hoskinson and Jr. because abbreviated titles following a person's name are set off by commas. You should know, however, that many writers choose not to set off the titles Jr. or Sr.)

126 ▶

A. Francis R. Kendall, M.D.,   Tulsa, Oklahoma,   OEO. (Did you remember the commas around the abbreviated title M.D.? Also, don't forget the comma after the state.)
B. April 15, 1979, Jimmy Carter,   U.S.,   450,000   day.

127 ▶

A. Mrs. Louise J. Hampton, D.D.S.,   Cherryville, Pennsylvania,   president/   A/D/A.
(The American Dental Association writes its abbreviated name as the ADA.)

128

B. Miss Kayla Rivera, M.D.
19826 Krenshaw Ave.
Springlake, N/J// 07762-4700   (Did you remember that the two-letter state abbreviation has no periods nor a comma before the ZIP Code?)

A. Baldwin and Willis, Ltd.
B. Davis, Decker, and Devereaux, Inc.
Notice in the example of this instructional frame that when the ampersand ("and" sign), is used in a company name, no comma should precede the ampersand—Bateman, James & Klausmeier, Ltd.)

129

130

A. Ltd.,   Liverpool, England,
B. Ashley, Inc.,

131

A. Grace Sheek & Sons, Ltd.
B. Deaver, Hibler, and Stevens, Inc., and DeWeese-McFaddin, Ltd.

The Justine/ Corporation/ merged with the Uston/ Company to become Just-Us, Inc., in 1989.

▸ 132

C) (Again, in Sentence D no comma should precede the ampersand; however, a comma should be placed after Ltd.)

▸ 133

Emma Moon, Ph.D., Juanita Kliendienst, M.A., Joe Lynch, D.D.S., and Harold Skaggs, Jr., flew to Auckland, New Zealand, Brisbane, Australia, and Jakarta, Indonesia, on Tuesday, June 20.
NOTE: Semicolons could be used after New Zealand and Australia for easier reading.

▸ 134

The following companies hired new resource personnel for the/, 1990/, expansion program: Pierpont Industries, Inc., added Gladys Brown, contracts administrator; the Holly/, Corporation of Birmingham, Alabama, employed Richard Wade, Jr., administrative assistant, formerly of the General Electric/, Company; and Adams/, and Adams, Ltd., hired Percey Lipton, Sr., and Glenda Symington/, as/, electrical engineers.   (Whew! Did you make it?)

▸ 135

end

▸ 136

137 Yours truly, (Only the first word of a complimentary close is capitalized.)

138

If the title is placed on another line, no comma is used to separate the name and title in the typed signature lines.

139 C. (Because all titles are placed on a separate line, none would use a comma to separate the person's name from his or her title. In Sentence B a comma would be correct *before* Jr., of course.)

140

Dear Miss Jodzko:
Yours sincerely,
NOTE: D.S. stands for double space. A double space always follows a salutation and precedes a complimentary close in a letter.

Both   (But please use mixed punctuation in this instructional program unless instructed to use open punctuation.)

141 ▶

Dolly, (or Dear Dolly:)

142 ▶

Dear Mr. Blackstone: (A colon is always proper unless open punctuation is requested. A comma is not normally used in a formal business letter. A semicolon is definitely wrong.)

143 ▶

No   (A comma is appropriate only after a first name.)

144 ▶

Dear Ms. Perez,	Incorrect	(Use a colon after a formal salutation.)
Dear Joe,	Correct	(or Dear Joe:)
Dear Hank:	Correct	(or Dear Hank,)
Dear Sirs and Madams;	Incorrect	(Never use a semicolon after any salutation.)

145 ▶

146

(A.) (B.) (A. & B.)

147

No punctuation following this salutation   (The colon after the salutation and the comma after the complimentary close would be omitted in open punctuation.)

148

mixed   a colon   salutation   a comma   complimentary close

149

Dear Ms. Wilson:
. . . .
             Sincerely yours,

Section 3

150

Both dependent and independent clauses can contain a subject and a verb, but only the independent clause will express a complete thought. A dependent clause "depends" on the rest of the sentence for its meaning.

Which part of the following sentence is independent? _____

               (1 or 2)

     1   2

[Even when something appears to be free], [someone is paying for it].

151

Circle the letter of the clause below that is incomplete (dependent) in meaning:

 A. A will is a set of legal instructions
 B. Even though a will is set of legal instructions

152

Underline the dependent clause and circle the independent clause in the sentence below:

 [As inflation decreases], [saving and investing become more attractive].

153

Independent clauses are also called <u>main</u> clauses. Since the dependent clause will always depend upon the independent clause for its full meaning, the independent clause is the <u>main</u> clause.

Underline the main clause once and the dependent clause twice:

 [An oligopoly exists] [when only a few businesses dominate a market].

154

Main clauses and _____ clauses are the same thing — they (can/cannot) stand alone because they are (complete/incomplete) in meaning.

155

Underline the dependent clauses below:

 A. [We must increase our level of productivity] [if we want to have a real increase in our standard of living].
 B. [Through the collection of sums of money called premiums], [mutual insurance companies invest and pay dividends back to the insured].

As you have probably noticed, dependent clauses may come at the beginning, the middle, or the end of a sentence.

Circle the letter of the sentence below which begins with a dependent clause:

  A. Scarcity exists when the demand for a particular commodity exceeds the supply of that item.
  B. When the demand for goods and services is greater than the supply, inflation typically occurs.

156 ▶

Rule No. 14

Use a comma to separate a dependent clause which has been shifted from its "normal" position to introduce the sentence.

  Normal position: Gold prices can fluctuate drastically and quickly if money markets are unstable.

  Shifted position: If money markets are unstable, gold prices can fluctuate drastically and quickly.

In the above example, "If money markets are unstable" is the _____ clause because it cannot stand alone. "Gold prices can fluctuate drastically and quickly" is a complete thought; therefore, it is called the _____ clause.

157 ▶

Which dependent clause has been shifted from its normal position?

_____
(A/B/Both/Neither)

  A. If you are like most people, you don't have the financial resources to satisfy all your needs and wants.
  B. Since human economic desires are unlimited, only some of those desires can be fulfilled.

158 ▶

Underline the dependent clauses:

  A. Although minors usually cannot be held liable for their contracts, they may be responsible for contracts dealing with necessities such as clothing, food, or shelter.
  B. If the severe weather persists, area schools will probably be closed.

159 ▶

Are the dependent clauses in the preceding frame in their normal position? _____
(Yes/No)

160 ▶

161

Circle the entire dependent clause below that is in its normal position:

A. Since payment notices are sent each month, the customer cannot forget to pay the installment.

B. Your local credit bureau can be an important contact if you are new to a city.

162

No response is required for this frame. Please read the following paragraph carefully:

One of the most common dependent clauses is the *introductory* clause. This clause will contain a subject and a verb but will be dependent upon the remainder of the sentence which follows (the independent clause) for its meaning. Introductory dependent clauses commonly begin with the following words although there are many others:

after	since
although	unless
as	when
because	while

163

As previously stated, introductory dependent clauses usually require a comma, whereas the same clause placed in its normal position (not at the beginning) does not require a comma.

Ex.: 1. **As the profit incentives increased, worker productivity went up significantly.**
2. **Worker productivity went up significantly_ as the profit incentives increased.**

A comma is used after the <u>as</u> clause in the first example because _____ _____. No comma is used before the <u>as</u> clause in the second example because _____.

164

Place a check mark beside the sentence below which contains a dependent clause:

_____ A. Typically financial planners recommend that the family's main wage earner have life insurance equal to six times annual income.

_____ B. Government spending is generally increased during periods of recession when the economy needs a boost.

165

Rewrite Sentence B in the previous frame so that the dependent clause will require a comma.

If the (dependent/independent) clause comes at the beginning of the sentence, commas (are/are not) used to set it off.

166

Punctuate at the points indicated if commas are needed:

If all resources of an economy are in use_ additional output of a certain product can be obtained_ if less of something else is produced.

167

Punctuate these sentences:

A. When investors know their individual goals they can decide which types of investments will best help them reach their goals.
B. As the United States grew into a highly complex economic system consumer problems of many kinds emerged.

168

Punctuate at all points where a comma is needed:

A. If used wisely installment buying can be of benefit to the consumer to business and to the economy in general.
B. A good credit rating must be earned and maintained if one wants to get credit when it is needed.

169

If the dependent clause at the beginning of the sentence is very short, the comma is optional although preferably omitted. If the clause is longer than three or four words, however, the comma is needed.

Short: <u>If</u> possible call me this afternoon.
Long: <u>Because</u> of Myra's ability and determination, she graduated with honors.

Would the sentence below need a comma? _____
(Yes/No)

Because of you the company increased its net income.

170

Place a check mark beside the introductory clause that would <u>not</u> require a comma:

_____ A. While exercising you should not strain to the point of pain.
_____ B. Once the public overcame its fear of a recession stock prices slowly started to rise again.

171

172

Underline the dependent clause and punctuate the sentence:

Monopoly exists in the market economy when a single seller provides the entire supply of a good or service.

173

Which sentence needs a comma? _____
(A/B/Both/Neither)

A. As it is I am not able to sell my wheat at the current price.
B. As a safeguard most canceled checks should be kept for a minimum of a year.

174

Place brackets around the dependent clause in this sentence:

Few of us are ever completely satisfied no matter how much we have.

Ask yourself the following questions: What part of the sentence expresses a complete thought (is independent)? What part depends upon the main clause for its meaning (is dependent)?

175

Place brackets around the two dependent clauses which introduce this sentence:

Because of the competitive nature of business, if retailers cannot obtain what they want from one wholesaler, there usually is another distributor who is more than happy to satisfy them.

176

No response is required for this frame. Read the review material that follows:

You know the following:
1. An independent clause expresses a complete thought; a dependent clause does not.
2. A dependent clause that introduces a sentence will usually be set off by a comma.
3. A dependent clause that falls in its normal position <u>after</u> the main clause normally is not punctuated.
4. Some of the most common introductory dependent clauses begin with words such as *if, when, while, because, although, since,* etc.
5. A short introductory clause does not require a comma; however, the writer has the option of using or not using a comma.

Insert punctuation as needed:

A. Because it is convenient and often is a means of adjusting high and low points in spending credit is used by people at all income levels.

B. The economy of the United States has been called a credit economy because the use of credit is so widespread.

▶ 177

Punctuate these sentences:

A. All entrepreneurs are rebels and mavericks to some extent since they possess personality traits that compel them to strike out on their own.

B. Economics is the study of a process that involves making choices as people try to get the greatest satisfaction when they purchase goods and services.

▶ 178

Punctuate:

A. If a high rate of return is desired an investor cannot expect a great degree of safety of principal.

B. When there is a rising level of prices without a corresponding increase in production inflation is nearly impossible to contain.

▶ 179

Even a short introductory clause should have a comma if the sentence could cause confusion or delay in understanding without a comma.

Wrong: Unless you do the chores of the organization will not get done.
Right: Unless you do, the chores of the organization will not get done.

Would the following short introductory clause require a comma? _____
(Yes/No)

Although I helped you and everyone else were certainly instrumental.

▶ 180

Circle the letter of the sentence with the short introductory clause that would be confusing without a comma:

A. If you can eat the whole watermelon because I don't have room for it in the refrigerator.

B. After college I am planning to work as an accountant.

▶ 181

182

The comma after a short introductory clause is usually _____

(required/optional)

The comma after a short introductory clause that could cause misunderstanding is _____

(required/optional)

183

Punctuate the following sentences:

A. As in the U.S. government plays a very important role in the economy.
B. As a favor would you mind picking up my dry cleaning on your way home

184

Do you agree with the punctuation in the sentence below? _____

(Yes/No/Not sure)

When inflation threatens the Federal Reserve Board tightens credit.

185

How should this sentence be punctuated to prevent possible misunderstanding?

When you do something dreadful always happens to bring you back to reality.

186

Other types of dependent clauses should also be set off by commas when they <u>introduce</u> the sentence. Participial phrases, infinitive phrases, a long prepositional phrase, or a series of short prepositional phrases are examples.

1. Participial: <u>Hoping</u> that it was not too late, the government took steps to halt the slide of the dollar.

2. Infinitive: <u>To</u> assure that social security would be solvent, the government raised the social security tax by ½ percent.

3. Long   <u>Among</u> the many alternatives that could have been chosen, the com-
   Prepositional: pany decided to do a buy-back of its own stock.

4. Series of   <u>About</u> the middle <u>of</u> its session <u>during</u> the past month, Congress passed
   Prepositionals: the foreign aid bill.

Participles usually end in _____; infinitive phrases start with the word _____; and a prepositional phrase or a series of prepositional phrases has to be very _____ to require a comma.

Underline the participial and infinitive phrases in these sentences and punctuate each sentence:

    A. Realizing that she could no longer make enough commissions the broker left Wall Street to start her own business.

    B. To alleviate the hazard of uncontrolled monopolies in this country the federal government passed a series of antitrust laws.

187 ▶

Circle the letter of the sentence below that would need a comma after the prepositional phrases:

    A. In a capitalistic economy the "oil" that keeps the wheels of progress turning is profit.

    B. In a capitalistic economy during times of severe recession unemployment may rise by 15 or 20 percentage points or higher.

188 ▶

You should make a significant purchase on credit when you move to a new community to establish your credit in that locality.

The sentence above contains _____ (how many?) main clause(s) and _____ (how many?) dependent clause(s).

189 ▶

Rewrite the sentence in Frame 189 so that the adverbial clause (starting with the word *when*) introduces the sentence:

_____

_____

190 ▶

Rewrite the sentence in Frame 189 so that the infinitive phrase (starting with the word *to*) introduces the sentence:

_____

_____

191 ▶

Just as with other dependent clauses, if an infinitive or participial phrase falls in its normal position (does not introduce the sentence), no commas are usually required.

Punctuate the following sentences:

    A. The broker left Wall Street to start her own business after realizing that she could no longer make enough commissions.

    B. The federal government passed a series of antitrust laws to alleviate the hazard of uncontrolled monopolies in this country.

192 ▶

193

Punctuate these sentences wherever commas are needed:

A. When comparing the same or similar policies of different companies do not compare cost alone.
B. Do not compare cost alone when comparing the same or similar policies of different companies.

194

As in short dependent clauses, very short participial, infinitive, or prepositional phrases that introduce the sentence do not require commas if no confusion exists.

Circle the letter of the sentence below that would need a comma:

A. In 1935 the U.S. Government started the social security system.
B. To compensate for the cost of goods stolen by a few dishonest people businesses must charge all customers higher prices.

195

Punctuate at the points indicated if necessary:

A. In socialistic economies_ the government owns and operates critical basic industries.
B. While paddling_ the swimmer lost his rhythm and his sense of direction.
C. To stay_ I would need to have some assurance that the company plans to hire additional personnel next year.

196

A typical comma mistake is the subject/verb split. Be careful when punctuating introductory expressions because the introductory clause may be the subject of the sentence. VERY IMPORTANT: A main (independent) clause must follow the introductory expression before the phrase can be set off with commas.

Ex.: 1. **Giving to charity is one way of reducing income taxes.**
2. **To protect and aid those who cannot help themselves is the goal of social legislation.**

In the above examples does a main clause follow the introductory expressions? _____ Can such introductory expressions be set off by commas when they act
(Yes/No)
as the subject of the sentence? _____
(Yes/No)

197

The sentence below begins with an infinitive phrase. Does it contain an independent clause after the phrase? _____
(Yes/No)

To collect legitimate taxes owed to the government is the function of the IRS.
Should a comma be used after the word government? _____
(Yes/No)

Place brackets around the infinitive phrases below; then punctuate the infinitive phrase(s) that should have a comma:

A. To make their purchasing decisions was the goal the teenagers had set for themselves.
B. To make their purchasing decisions they must rely on the information advertisers have provided.
C. They must rely on the information advertisers have provided to make their purchasing decisions.

198 ▶

Watch for review as you punctuate these sentences:

A. By fulfilling the needs and wants of people businesses are able to make a profit.
B. In making important economic decisions a person should recognize the true opportunity cost.

199 ▶

Punctuate:

A. To pay for their high costs of billing credit card companies often charge rates of 18 percent or higher since most people don't pay off their balances when due.
B. Even if free public transportation probably wouldn't rid our cities entirely of air pollution problems.

200 ▶

Rule No. 15

Parenthetical expressions, often called interrupters because they "interrupt" the natural flow of the sentence, are usually set off by commas. Such expressions are not necessary for grammatical completeness and can be omitted without changing the basic meaning of the sentence.

Underscore the "interrupting" phrase in the following sentence and punctuate:

Our economic system there can be no doubt is not a pure capitalistic system.

201 ▶

In which sentence below can you omit the material set off by commas and still have a sentence that is basically unchanged in meaning? _____
(A/B/Both/Neither)

202 ▶

A. Spending, needless to say, puts additional pressure on supplies and prices which adds to inflation.
B. Most people, to be sure, save for their future wants and needs.

The word *parentheses* can be seen in the word *parenthetical*. Anything that can be placed in parentheses can be taken out of a sentence without impairing the meaning. <u>Long</u> parentheticals are placed in parentheses. <u>Short</u> parenthetical expressions, however, are set off by commas.

203

> Ex.: 1. **The Consumer Price Index (<u>it reflects changes in goods and services</u>) is issued monthly by the Bureau of Labor Statistics.**
> 2. **Your payment, <u>to say the least</u>, has been heartily received.**

Why is the parenthetical expression in the first example above placed in parentheses and the second example set off by commas?

204

A short parenthetical expression is not essential to the basic meaning of the sentence and is punctuated by commas to show that it interrupts and could be removed.

Is the underlined phrase below essential to the basic meaning? _____

(Yes/No)

A franchise <u>as you may know</u> is a right to operate a business in a specified geographic location.

205

Circle the letter of the sentence below which has an interrupter that can be omitted without altering the basic meaning:

A. Automation_ by using the combination of known inventions_ brings about automatic control of a production process.

B. Automation has_ without a doubt_ been a creator of jobs.

206

Punctuate the parenthetical expression that introduces this sentence:

For example in the opening paragraph of good-news letters, try to indicate the purpose for writing.

207

The most common single-word parenthetical expressions are words like *however, therefore, nevertheless,* and *furthermore.* Multiple-word parenthetical expressions are almost limitless: *For example, in general, in fact, in other words, needless to say, without a doubt,* and *of course* are only a few illustrations.

Underline the two parenthetical expressions in the following sentences and punctuate them: (What words can be taken out without altering the basic meaning of the sentence?)

In other words the main purpose of taxation without a doubt is to provide services that only collectively we could afford.

Long parenthetical expressions are usually placed in parentheses rather than punctuated by commas.

Would Sentence A or Sentence B below need parentheses around the parenthetical?

208

    A. Economics on the other hand is a science that attempts to explain how societies deal with complicated economic issues.

    B. Ownership in a corporation corporations are formed by state charter is represented by shares of stock.

Are the words in brackets in the sentence below a parenthetical expression? _____
                                                        (Yes/No)

209

[Without free public education] we would not enjoy such a literate populace.

The test of a parenthetical expression is that if it is omitted:

    A. the sentence is no longer a sentence.
    B. the sentence remains a sentence, but the meaning is changed.
    C. the sentence is not a sentence even though the meaning is unchanged.
    D. the sentence remains a sentence, and the meaning is not changed.

210

Which of the above statements is true? _____
                                         (A/B/C/D/None)

Does either of these sentences contain a parenthetical expression? _____
                                             (Yes/No)

211

    A. The act_ passed in 1927_ has remained unchanged.
    B. The jurist changed her vote_ without giving a reason.

As you have seen, a parenthetical expression can be one word or several words; it can come at the beginning, the middle, or the end of a sentence.

Punctuate the interrupters in these sentences:

212

    A. In general people in the U.S. save about half as much as people in Japan.
    B. People in the U.S. as a matter of fact typically save about 6 to 8 percent of their income.
    C. About 15 percent of income is saved in Japan however.

213

Each of these sentences contains two parentheticals. Punctuate them:

A. The basic problem as a matter of fact is the principle of scarcity—more wants needless to say than resources can supply.

B. By the way most families give up trying to make a budget because their budget without a doubt is too complicated.

214

Punctuate these sentences:

A. Today's workers in case you didn't know can produce over five times more goods than a worker could produce at the beginning of this century.

B. Collateral to be sure will be necessary in qualifying for a loan.

C. Change for the sake of change is foolish; to remain at the status quo because we feel secure is just as foolish however.

215

Use a comma to set off such words as *yes, no, well*, etc., when they begin a sentence or clause and when they are meant to be read as parenthetical expressions.

Underline any parentheticals in the following sentence:

No, I have no desire to go to the state university.

216

Punctuate the parenthetical expressions:

A. Yes the average American family spends about 25 to 30 percent of its income on housing.

B. Well who could have foreseen that information would become the largest single industry in this country?

217

Does the sentence below contain a parenthetical expression? _____
                                                              (Yes/No)

The director said yes to the proposal.

218

Circle the letter of the sentence which contains a parenthetical:

A. <u>Well</u> the president is certainly liked by everyone.

B. Everyone certainly thinks <u>well</u> of the president.

Punctuate any parentheticals in this sentence:

No education should end with a high school diploma, but it should continue throughout life.

▶ **219**

Punctuate the sentence below to show that cigarettes are okay for your health:

No_ cigarettes are harmful to your health.

Punctuate the sentence again arguing that cigarettes should not be used:

No_ cigarettes are harmful to your health.

▶ **220**

Statements of direct address are normally considered to be parentheticals. Therefore, when speaking to someone directly, use commas to set off the person's name.

Ex.: 1. **Barbara, why do you insist on doing everything your own way?**
2. **I have to know now, Dad, if I can have the car tonight!**

Circle the word below that is a direct address and insert any needed punctuation:

Did you know Marian that inflationary pressures in the economy tend to be created by both unjustified wage increases and monopolistic price increases?

▶ **221**

Circle the letter of the sentence below which contains a direct address:

A. Did you know Steve, the delivery boy?
B. Could you let me know as soon as possible, Janice.

▶ **222**

Punctuate these sentences:

A. As you may know money is anything that is generally used to pay for the purchase of goods and services and to pay debts.
B. A promissory note without a doubt would be the smartest way to handle the transaction.

▶ **223**

Students often think that every time they see such words as *therefore, however, no doubt, of course,* and other common parentheticals, they should insert commas. Not so! Commas are used *only* when these words are interrupters. Sometimes the writer doesn't intend the short parenthetical to interrupt.

Consider these examples:

224

> **Ex.: 1. You've no doubt heard of supercomputers.**
> **2. You are therefore entitled to the largest discount possible.**

Why are the above examples not punctuated? (Circle the letter of the correct answer.)

A. The sentences contain no parentheticals.
B. The parentheticals are too short to require commas.
C. The writer probably did not intend the parentheticals to interrupt.
D. The parentheticals are too long and should be placed in parentheses.

225

Is the word *However* intended to be an interrupter in the following sentence? _____
(Yes/No)

However you invest your money will not affect my decision.

Sometimes a sentence or an independent clause begins with an expression that links it to the preceding thought. These links are **conjunctions** and come at the beginning of the second sentence or clause.

226

> **Ex.: 1. We must have the information by Friday. <u>Therefore</u>, could you please call as soon as you receive this letter.**
> **2. I doubt it; <u>however</u>, I will take your word for it.**

Circle the linking expressions in these sentences:

A. Nevertheless, the real cost of any choice is what a person must give up in order to gain what is wanted.
B. A rebound in real estate is very likely; however, in the next couple of years, the market is expected to be soft.

227

Punctuate the sentence below which contains an introductory linking word.

A. However real friends might seem to be, they sometimes let you down.
B. However real friends are hard to find.

Rule No. 16

The information in this frame is a continuation of Frame 226. Please read on very carefully.

Use a comma after introductory expressions such as *of course, however, accordingly, after all, therefore,* or other introductory expressions when they are used as conjunctions to connect one thought to a preceding thought.

Punctuate the linking words (conjunctions) in these sentences:

A. Median family incomes have increased. Nevertheless in real terms (adjusting for inflation) salaries have declined.

B. Under Workmen's Compensation, injured workers are entitled to benefits for injuries resulting from accidents; however states vary as to the nature of the laws governing this business practice.

228

A complete thought will always follow a linking expression (conjunction). Otherwise, the phrase is not a linking expression and should *not* be set off by commas.

One sentence below contains a linking expression. Circle the linking expression and punctuate each sentence:

A. However_ local taxes are spent will ultimately determine the quality of life in this city.

B. In addition_ the balance of trade is improving every quarter.

229

Punctuate the conjunctions (linking expressions) in each of these sentences:

A. Public utilities are natural monopolies; however they are regulated by state and federal governments.

B. Of course all financial markets are becoming more international.

230

Which sentence has the linking expression properly punctuated? _____
(A/B/Both/Neither)

A. Thus most state taxes help to construct and to improve highways.

B. The federal government tries to spend its money on projects that are in the national interest; of course it does not always succeed.

231

A conjunction is used to connect two independent clauses or two sentences. A parenthetical expression does not connect anything; it merely provides additional information that can be left out without changing the basic meaning.

232

> Ex.: 1. We wondered, <u>however</u>, if decisions should be made centrally or decentrally.
> 2. An increase in prices hurts those whose incomes are fixed; <u>therefore</u>, those with fixed incomes benefit by a fall in prices.

Which of the above examples has two main clauses? _____

(Ex. 1 or Ex. 2)

In Example 1 the word *however* is used as a _____ .
In Example 2 the word *therefore* is used as a _____ .

233

Circle a letter below to correctly complete the following statement:

If the conjunction *therefore* connects two independent clauses, a comma will

    A. precede the conjunction.
    B. follow the conjunction.
    C. precede and follow the conjunction.

234

Circle a letter below to correctly complete the following statement:

If a parenthetical expression occurs in the middle of a sentence, a comma will

    A. precede the expression.
    B. follow the expression.
    C. precede and follow the expression.

235

Almost any conjunction at the beginning of a sentence or a main clause will be followed by a comma if the intent is to make a transition from one thought to another.

> Ex.: Our sale begins Thursday. Indeed, you will want to be one of the first to arrive at the store.

Punctuate the following sentence:

> Accordingly all those who have been with the company for ten years or more will have the option of staying here or moving to the new location.

Watch for review as you punctuate the sentences that follow:

A. The D O T (Dictionary of Occupational Titles) lists nearly 40000 (forty thousand) titles which describe jobs that people hold. However technology creates new job titles every year

B. Wage increases in the U S however ranged between 3 and 5 percent a year during most of the 1980s

236 ▶

Watch for review as you insert punctuation wherever needed:

A. We have to know therefore by Monday July 25 whether or not you will accept the offer

B. To be sure one of the skills most needed by office workers today is so we've heard the ability to compose at the computer terminal

237 ▶

Place a comma at the points indicated if one is required:

A. We cannot_ accept your order_ after May 1_ however.

B. We will help you_ all we can. Of course_ if you don't need much help_ I'm sure_ that someone else could use the scholarship.

238 ▶

Circle the letter of the sentence below in which the writer probably did not intend an interruption in the flow of the sentence:

A. Therefore_ I am forced to void the contract.

B. We_ therefore_ ask that you refrain from dumping industrial waste into our rivers, lakes, and streams.

C. We decided_ therefore_ that yours was the best offer.

239 ▶

Punctuate this sentence:

Well Nancy Marcia and Mike just to name a few are examples of the high-calibre student at this school.

240 ▶

Circle the letter of the sentence below that is correctly punctuated:

A. Actually, her modesty was overwhelming; however I could see that she was embarrassed.

B. Yes, I did check with the superintendent, sir.

241 ▶

242

Which of the sentences below is punctuated correctly? _____

(A/B/Both/Neither)

A. Yes, two-thirds of the world's people, I'm sorry to say, live in underdeveloped nations.
B. Fortunately, I might add, Henry, world production rose 6 percent last year .

243

Should the following sentence have a comma at the point indicated? _____

(Yes/No)

Be sure to let us know_ if you think you will be able to go.

(See Frames 163 and 164 if you don't remember.)

244

Punctuate the following sentences:

A. Your order we can assure you Mr Bonn will take the top priority on our list
B. I do of course try to avoid starting a business letter with *I*; consequently a *you* attitude is easier to achieve
C. Are you ready for college Liz

This is the end of Section 3. How are you doing so far? If you find that after working on the material for a long period of time you can't concentrate, you should stop for a while and do something else. When you return to the material, you may then find that you are ready to pursue your self-teaching with renewed vigor.

Take the section test following the directions given in Section 1. After you have inserted all marks of punctuation, turn the page and check yourself. The final page is for your review; it lists all the items in the test by number and tells you in what frame you can review the item. These section tests not only let you check yourself on the material in the immediate section, but they also review all the material in previous sections. Be sure to go back and look up any items that you missed before continuing to Section 4.

BUSINESS MEMORANDUM

TO: Sam Potter Sales Manager
FROM: G L Gooding
DATE: October 22 19__
SUBJ: Our annual appraisal by corporate headquarters

As you know on Wednesday November 10 Mr C M Kalinski corporate vice president will be visiting our St Louis office(E) Yes this is the day Sam that we have all been eagerly awaiting(E) However are we ready(E) This past month without a doubt has been hectic; and because of forces beyond everyone's control we may not be as ready as we should be(E)

Having been out of the office so much myself during October I was wondering if you could take the lead this time in handling all details(E) If so I would be terribly relieved to say the least(E) However you wish to handle everything will be fine with me(E) To show Mr Kalinski that we are still the top producers of the five regions we should in my opinion generate several impressive performance reports that go back 5 10 and even 15 years(E) No doubt he has been impressed by specific facts in the past when we have had to defend our unorthodox marketing procedures and maintain our No 1 status in the company(E)

Nevertheless the past our track record is exemplary of course is history(E) This year will be tougher than any other I can guarantee it(E) Since your division is one of our star performers Sam you may want to review February April and July with him in great detail(E) Indeed those months were exceptional for us don't you agree(E)

Depending on the outcome of his visit I predict furthermore that all of us will be in a better position to move forward even more dramatically next year(E) Good luck my friend in meeting this challenge(E) I know you will rise to the occasion in grand style as you always do(E) Let me know what any of us in this office can do to help(E) Obviously we all have our reputations at stake and our futures(E)

---

*NOTE: The above communication exercise obviously contains far too much punctuation, especially interrupters. However, in order to get the practice you need, the copy must be heavily "loaded" (contrived) to provide as broad a coverage of key punctuation as possible in the shortest amount of time.

TO: Sam Potter[1], Sales Manager
FROM: G. L. Gooding 𝓐.𝓐.
DATE: October 22, 19__
SUBJ: Our annual appraisal by corporate headquarters

As you know[5], on Wednesday[6], November 10[7], Mr. C. M. Kalinski[11], corporate vice president[12], will be visiting our St. Louis office[13]. Yes, this is the day, Sam, that we have all been eagerly awaiting[18*]! However[19], are we ready[20]? This past month[21], without a doubt[22], has been hectic; and because of forces beyond everyone's control[23], we may not be as ready as we should be[24].

Having been out of the office so much myself during October[25], I was wondering if you could take the lead this time in handling all details[26]. If so[27*] I would be terribly relieved[28], to say the least[29]. However[30] you wish to handle everything will be fine with me[31]. To show Mr. Kalinski[32] that we are still the top producers of the five regions[33], we should[34], in my opinion[35], generate several impressive performance reports that go back 5[36], 10[37*], and even 15 years[38]. No doubt[39*] he has been impressed by specific facts in the past[40] when we have had to defend our unorthodox marketing procedures[41] and maintain our No. 1 status in the company[43].

Nevertheless[44], the past[45] (our track record is exemplary[46], of course[47]) is history[48]. This year will be tougher than any other[49], I can guarantee it[50]. Since your division is one of our star performers[51], Sam[52], you may want to review February[53], April[54*], and July with him in great detail[55]. Indeed[56], those months were exceptional for us[57], don't you agree[58]?

Depending on the outcome of his visit[59], I predict[60], furthermore[61], that all of us[62] will be in a better position to move forward even more dramatically next year[63]. Good luck[64*], my friend[65], in meeting this challenge[66]. I know you will rise to the occasion in grand style[67] as you always do[68]. Let me know what any of us in this office can do to help[69*]. Obviously[70*], we all have our reputations at stake and our futures.

The * after the mark of punctuation indicates that the punctuation at this point is optional or that the punctuation is dependent on the emphasis desired such as a period or exclamation point. Optional punctuation will be indicated by an * throughout the remainder of this text.

---

*NOTE: The above communication exercise obviously contains far too much punctuation, especially interrupters. However, in order to get the practice you need, the copy must be heavily "loaded" (contrived) to provide as broad a coverage of key punctuation as possible in the shortest amount of time.

REVIEW SHEETS

If you missed Number	See Frame Number	Practice Sentence
1	119	
2	15	
3	15	
4	97	
5	162, 163	
6	97	
7	97	
8	15	
9	15	
10	15	
11	119	
12	119	
13	15	
14	2	
15	215	
16	221	
17	221	
18	6	
19	226, 228	
20	10	
21	201, 203	
22	201, 203	
23	162, 163	
24	2	
25	186	
26	10	
27	170	
28	201, 204	
29	2	
30	229	
31	2	

If you missed Number	See Frame Number	Practice Sentence
32	15	_____
33	186	_____
34	201, 203	_____
35	204	_____
36	57	_____
37	57, 59	_____
38	2	_____
39	201	_____
40	157, 163	_____
41	64, 68	_____
42	15	_____
43	2	_____
44	226, 228	_____
45	203	_____
46	201, 207	_____
47	203	_____
48	2	_____
49	201, 212	_____
50	2	_____
51	221, 157, 162	_____
52	221	_____
53	57	_____
54	57, 59	_____
55	2	_____
56	226, 228	_____
57	201, 212	_____
58	10	_____
59	186	_____
60	207, 201, 204	_____
61	207, 201, 204	_____
62	2	_____
63	221	_____
64	221	_____
65	2	_____
66	157, 163	_____

If you missed Number	See Frame Number	Practice Sentence
67	2	_____
68	2	_____
69	228	_____
70	64	_____

2 (Read Clause 1. Does it express a complete thought? No. Then read Clause 2. Does it express a complete thought? Yes.)

150 ►

B.

151 ►

As inflation decreases, ⟨ saving and investing become more attractive. ⟩

152 ►

An oligopoly exists   when only a few businesses dominate a market.

153 ►

independent   can   complete

154 ►

A. if we want to have a real increase in our standard of living.
B. Through the collection of sums of money called premiums.

155 ►

B.

156

157

dependent
independent (or main)

158 Both   (They both introduce the sentence.)

159

A. Although minors usually cannot be held liable for their contracts,
B. If the severe weather persists,

160   No   (They introduce the sentence.)

(if you are new to a city) .

161

No response is needed.

162

it introduces the sentence.
it is in its normal position.

163

___✔___ B. ("when the economy needs a boost" is a dependent clause.)

164

When the economy needs a boost, government spending is generally increased during periods of recession.

165

166

dependent . . . are
independent . . . are not

167

<u>If</u> all resources of an economy are in use, (No comma would be placed after the word *ob-
tained* because the second *if* clause ends the sentence.)

168

A. When investors know their individual goals, . . .
B. As the United States grew into a highly complex economic system, . . .

169

A. If used wisely, to the consumer, to business, (Did you remember to punctuate the
series at the end of this sentence?)
B. None (The dependent clause is in its normal position.)

170

No, although some writers would use a comma. (The introductory dependent clause is probably short enough to omit the comma.)

171

_✔_ A.

when a single seller provides the entire supply of a good or service.   (No additional punctuation is needed because the dependent clause does not introduce the sentence.)

172 ▶

Neither   (However, keep in mind that some writers would use a comma, even here.)

173 ▶

[no matter how much we have]

174 ▶

[Because of the competitive nature of business],
[if retailers cannot obtain what they want from one wholesaler],

175 ▶

No response is needed.

176 ▶

177

A. Because it is convenient and . . . spending,   (This introductory dependent clause is quite a bit longer than the main clause at the end of the sentence.)

B. None   (The dependent clause is in its normal position at the end.)

178

A. None   (The dependent clause comes at the end.)

B. None   (The two dependent clauses at the end begin with *as* and *when.*)

179

A. If a high rate of return is desired, . . .

B. When there is . . . production, . . .

180

Yes   (Right: Although I helped, you and everyone else . . .
         Wrong: Although I helped you and everyone else . . .)

181

Ⓐ   If you can, eat the whole watermelon . . . <u>not</u> . . . If you can eat the whole watermelon . . .)

optional
required

182 ▶

A. As in the U.S., . . .   (Otherwise, U.S. and government would seem to go together.)
B. No comma after favor . . . home. (The clause is short and not confusing. Did you put a period at the end of the polite request?)

183 ▶

If you do agree, you had better reread Frame 180.

184 ▶

When you do,   (Otherwise, the reader might begin the sentence as follows: When you do something dreadful . . .)

185 ▶

ing
to
long

186 ▶

187

A. <u>Realizing that she could no longer make enough commissions,</u>   (*Realizing* is the participle.)
B. <u>To alleviate the hazard of uncontrolled monopolies in this country,</u>   (*To* is the infinitive.)

188

B. (A comma is needed after the word *recession* because the sentence has a series of introductory prepositional phrases. In Sentence A, a comma after the word economy would be optional but would probably be avoided by most writers.)

189

one
two   (The first dependent clause is <u>when you move to a new community</u>; the second dependent clause is <u>to establish your credit in that locality</u>.)

190

<u>When you move to a new community,</u> you should make a significant purchase on credit to establish your credit in that locality.

191

<u>To establish your credit in that locality,</u> when you move to a new community, you should make a signficant purchase on credit.

192

A. None   (The participial phrase comes after the main clause.)
B. None   (The infinitive phrase does not introduce the sentence.)

NOTE: Please reread Frame 186 to contrast the use of a comma after an introductory participle or infinitive phrase.

A. companies,   (The dependent clause introduces the sentence.)
B. None   (The dependent clause is in its normal position.)

193

B.)   (The short introductory prepositional phrase in Sentence A would require no comma.)

194

A. None   (No comma is necessary following a short introductory prepositional phrase.)
B. While paddling,   (*While paddling the swimmer* might be read without the comma.)
C. No comma is necessary, but one is optional.   (Punctuation is frequently left up to the judgment of the writer. This important concept cannot be overemphasized.)

195

No
No

196

No
No   (The infinitive phrase is the subject of the sentence.)

197

198

A. [To make their purchasing decisions]   (No comma)
B. [To make their purchasing decisions],   (The main clause follows, so the comma is needed.)
C.   . . . [to make their purchasing decisions].   (The dependent clause is in its normal position, so no comma is needed.)

199

A. people,
B. decisions,

200

A. billing,
B. free,   (Otherwise, misunderstanding could result.)

201

Our economic system, there can be no doubt,

202

Both   (Spending . . . puts additional pressure on supplies and prices which adds to inflation. Most people . . . save for their future wants and needs.)

The parenthetical expression in Sentence A is long.
The parenthetical expression in Sentence B is short.

VERY IMPORTANT: Good writers avoid placing interrupters in the middle of sentences as much as possible because interrupters impede the flow of reading. The examples in this text are given only for your practice.

203 ▶

No   (If you take out the phrase *as you may know,* the basic meaning of the sentence remains the same. Therefore, commas should be placed around this parenthetical.)

204 ▶

Ⓑ *(Automation has . . . been a creator of jobs* is the basic meaning.)

205 ▶

For example,_   (Do you remember why a comma would be placed after the word *letters?*)

206 ▶

<u>In other words</u>, the main purpose of taxation, <u>without a doubt,</u> . . .

207 ▶

B. (The parenthetical expression in Sentence A would be set off by commas.)

208

209

No (Even though a complete sentence or thought follows the brackets, the phrase is essential to the full meaning of the sentence.)

D. (Omitting a parenthetical expression leaves the sentence grammatically intact.)

210

No (In both cases you can take the phrase out and still have a complete sentence, <u>but</u> the basic meaning of the sentence is changed.)

211

A. In general,
B. , as a matter of fact,
C. , however.

212

A. , as a matter of fact, , needless to say,
B. By the way, , without a doubt, (A point of review: Notice that no comma is placed before the word *because* since this dependent clause is in its normal position.)

213 ▶

A. , in case you didn't know,
B. , to be sure,
C. , however. (The phrase *for the sake of change* is part of the basic meaning. The phrase *because we feel secure* does not introduce the clause.)

214 ▶

No,

215 ▶

A. Yes,
B. Well,

216 ▶

No (Take out the word *yes* and read the sentence. It doesn't make sense, does it?)

217 ▶

Ⓐ.

218 ▶

219 There is no parenthetical in this sentence.

220 No cigarettes are harmful to your health.
No, cigarettes are harmful to your health.

(You see, sometimes punctuation depends on the meaning you intend.)

221 Did you know, (Marian), (A comma should be placed before and after the name.)

222

223 A. As you may know, (Otherwise, *As you may know money* might be mistakenly read
together.)
B. A promissory note, without a doubt, would be . . .

C.

▶ **224**

No   (The clause *However you invest your money* is the subject of the sentence.)

▶ **225**

A. (Nevertheless),
B. (however),

▶ **226**

Sentence B contains an introductory linking word.
However, real friends are hard to find.

▶ **227**

228

A. Nevertheless,
B. however,

229

A. No linking expression; no punctuation
B. (In addition),

230

A. Public utilities are natural monopolies; however, . . .
B. Of course, . . .

231

Neither   (If you missed this question, please reread and rework Frames 226 and 228 very carefully.)

Ex. 2
parenthetical expression
conjunction (It <u>connects</u> or <u>links</u> the two independent clauses.)

232 ▶

B. (If you chose one of the other responses, you can't distinguish between a parenthetical expression and a conjunction. Do not continue working in this textbook until you are clear on the difference between the two.)

233 ▶

C. (If you got the last two frames correct, you are reading and working with understanding.)

234 ▶

Accordingly<u>,</u>

235 ▶

236

A. D.O.T.   40,000   However,   year.
B. U.S., however,   1980s.

237

A. , therefore,   Monday, July 25,   offer.
B. sure,   , so we've heard,   terminal.

238

A. May 1, however.
B. Of course,   help,

239

Ⓑ (The parenthetical in Sentence B could be punctuated with or without commas depending upon the writer's intent.)

240

Well, Nancy, Marcia, and Mike, just to name a few, are examples of the high-calibre student at this school.

241

Ⓑ (In Sentence A the word *however* should be followed by a comma.)

Both

242 ▶

No

243 ▶

A. Your order, we can assure you, Mr. Bonn,   list.
B. I do, of course,   consequently,   achieve.
C. Are you ready for college, Liz?

244 ▶

Section 4

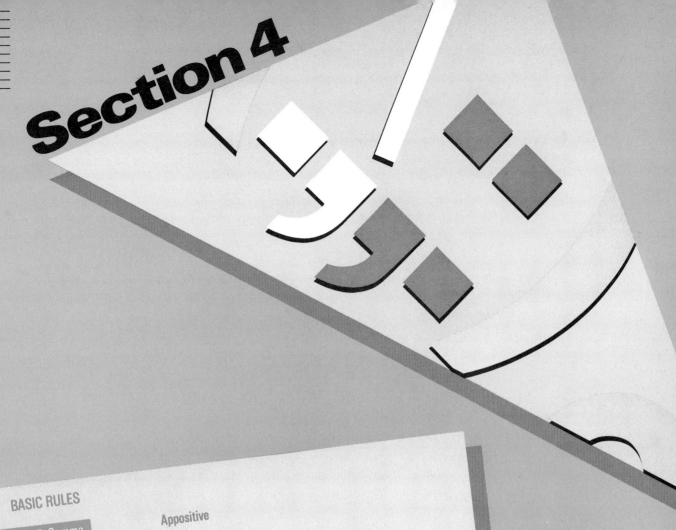

Rule No. 17

245

Another common interrupter besides the parenthetical expression is the *appositive*. An **appositive**, which renames or explains the noun or pronoun it modifies, can be omitted from the sentence without changing the meaning. Therefore, it is usually set off by commas.

Ex.: 1. New Orleans, the city of jazz, has a rich French heritage.
2. The fiduciary of the estate, Raymond Harrison, sought professional financial counseling.

In the first example above, "the city of jazz" is a(n) _____ modifying the proper noun _____. In the second example, the appositive _____ renames the noun phrase _____.

246

Circle the word or phrase (the appositive) that renames or describes the nouns in both sentences below:

A. Marketing channel, the path that a product travels from producer to consumer, is a complex network.
B. The more expensive type of insurance, whole life, has a cash value through a savings feature.

247

Because it renames or describes the noun or pronoun, an appositive will always (precede/follow) the noun or pronoun it modifies.

248

An appositive can be one word or several words. If the appositive merely renames the noun or gives some added information—but is not essential to the basic meaning of the sentence—it is set off by commas.

Punctuate the appositives in these sentences:

A. My only brother Steven serves in the United States Air Force.
B. Nearly 30 percent of the U.S. population over 66 million Americans receive some form of government aid.

249

Punctuate the two nonessential appositives in the sentence below:

Tennessee touched by eight states is the home of Elvis the king of rock and roll.

An appositive can modify either a single word (a noun or a pronoun) or a whole phrase.

Underline the phrases that the appositives modify in the sentences below and punctuate the appositives:

A. The Consumer Product Safety Commission created in 1972 has broad powers to protect the public from unsafe products.
B. The FTC established in 1915 works to preserve healthy competition in a free-market economy.

250

Appositives frequently begin with words like *usually* or *especially* or *particularly*. Treat these qualifiers the same way you do all nonessential appositives—put commas around them.

Punctuate these sentences:

A. A filing fee usually under $10 is charged.
B. Tax money especially money spent on national defense is allocated a year prior to actually being spent.
C. Consumers rely upon seals of approval particularly the Good Housekeeping Seal for making wise economic choices.

251

In the sentence below, underscore both appositives and punctuate them:

Tariffs sometimes known as customs duties are taxes levied on exports or imports usually the latter.

252

Circle the letter of the sentence(s) below that contain(s) a nonessential appositive:

A. The Truth in Lending Bill passed by Congress in 1968 requires that exact costs be spelled out to the borrower.
B. Information processing a term which includes all communication technologies is one of the fastest growing careers of the 1990s.

253

Punctuate any nonessential appositives in the sentences of Frame 253 above:

254

Circle the letter of the phrase below which correctly completes the following statement:

The test for a nonrestrictive (nonessential) appositive is that if it is omitted:

255

A. the sentence is no longer a sentence.
B. the sentence remains a sentence, but the meaning is changed.
C. the sentence remains a sentence, and the meaning is unchanged.
D. the sentence is not a sentence even though the meaning is unchanged.

256

An **essential appositive** is one that is needed to identify the noun or pronoun it modifies and thus complete the full meaning of the sentence.

Ex.: **The government agency OSHA handles all claims for occupational hazards.**

The government has hundreds of agencies; therefore, the appositive OSHA _____ the agency, rather than renames the agency.

257

A **nonessential appositive** merely renames or describes the noun or pronoun it modifies. An **essential appositive** actually identifies the noun or pronoun it modifies.

Which underlined appositive below answers the question <u>which one</u>? (Circle the letter of the sentence that would <u>not</u> be punctuated by commas.)

A. Economic growth a <u>creator of jobs</u> requires a continuous supply of capital.
B. The economist <u>John Kenneth Galbraith</u> wrote several best sellers.

258

Although most appositives are set off by commas, some are <u>essential</u>; that is, they <u>identify</u> the noun or pronoun and thus should not be punctuated.

Ex.: **Your friend <u>Thomas</u> made the Dean's List at Duquesne University.**

If you removed the appositive, the above example would not answer the crucial question
_____. It is therefore a(n) _____ appositive re-
                                                       (essential/nonessential)

quiring no commas.

259

Circle the letter of the sentence below which contains a nonessential appositive and insert the necessary punctuation:

A. The reference book *Best's Insurance Reports* is an excellent resource.
B. *Best's Insurance Reports* a reference work available in most libraries is an excellent resource.

Essential appositives are <u>not</u> set off by commas because they are needed to identify the noun or pronoun they modify. If you omitted them (commas around appositives mean you can take the material out), the meaning of the sentence would not be complete.

Punctuate the appositives in the following sentences:

> A. Aggregate demand the total demand of all people for goods and services produced by an economy is a part of macroeconomics.
> B. The senator Ted Kennedy never ran for president of the United States.

▶ **260**

How would you punctuate the appositive in this sentence? Why?

> The term <u>standard of living</u> is a measure of how well the people of a particular country live.

▶ **261**

If the appositive is needed to answer the question <u>which one</u>, commas (should/should not) be used. If the appositive could be removed without altering the meaning of the sentence, commas (should/should not) be used.

▶ **262**

The following sentence contains one essential and one nonessential appositive. Punctuate them.

> Chopin the greatest of all Polish composers wrote his composition Polonaise in G Minor when he was only seven years old.

▶ **263**

To determine if an appositive requires commas, ask yourself two questions:

> 1. Is there a possibility that there is _____?
> 2. Do I know _____?

▶ **264**

If the noun that the appositive modifies is specific, commas will almost always be used (nonessential).

> Specific: *This* partnership, owned by us, was formed three years ago.
> Nonspecific: The partnership owned by us was formed three years ago.
>
> In the first example the word _____ identifies which partnership.
> In the second example no commas are used around the appositive because _____
> _____.

▶ **265**

A proper noun, such as a person's name, will almost always be specific. Put commas around the appositive following a proper noun if the identity of the proper noun is known.

266

Ex.: 1. **Brian Boitano, national figure skating champion, won the gold medal at the Calgary Winter Olympics.**
2. **The Consumer Price Index, a monthly index of the average change in prices of a fixed group of goods and services, has been used since 1919.**

In the examples above, the words *Brian Boitano* and *Consumer Price Index* are
_____. The commas around the appositives make the appositives
(proper nouns/appositives)

_____.
(essential/nonessential)

267

Remember, the essential appositive must <u>identify</u> the noun it modifies. If it merely gives additional information but does not help to identify <u>which one</u>, the appositive will be nonessential.

Punctuate these appositives:

A. National debt the amount of money owed by the federal government has increased at a slower rate than the economy's growth.
B. Linda's sister Katherine was appointed chairperson.
C. Proprietorship a form of business in which one individual owns the entire business is the easiest type of business to create.

268

Circle the letter of the sentence below which contains a nonessential appositive; then underscore each appositive in each sentence:

A. The corporation 3M has been a large conglomerate for over 30 years.
B. The corporation which we talked about in class last Friday is created by a state charter.

269

Punctuate these appositives:

A. Disposable income the money that is left over after taxes actually declined during the past decade.
B. A bond a liability to a corporation is a loan from an individual for a specified number of years.

270

Find the appositives in the following sentences and punctuate them:

A. Gross national product the value of the total quantities of all goods and services produced can be measured in current prices.
B. Monopolies regulated by governments have appointed governing boards.

Sometimes an essential appositive with just a slight change in wording can be made nonessential and vice versa. Only by reading the sentence carefully for its full meaning can you tell whether the appositive is needed for complete meaning. In other words, punctuation is often determined by _____.
        (rule/judgment)

271

Place a check mark beside the sentence below that should have the nonessential appositive set off by commas:

_____ A. The administrative assistant Ms. Rebecca Cohen was promoted to records manager.

_____ B. Ms. Rebecca Cohen an administrative assistant was promoted to records manager.

272

Underline the <u>four</u> appositives in the following paragraph and insert the necessary punctuation: (Be careful—think about what you have learned.)

1   The term credit means the present use of future income. It allows the
2   consumer to have the use of goods and services before actually paying
3   for them. Credit a service for which a consumer pays should be used only
4   in amounts that can comfortably be repaid out of future income. A person
5   should never incur a debt especially one that could cause bankruptcy
6   unless there is a clear way to repay the debt. Credit is a privilege,
7   and the way to use it wisely is to shop around for a loan. The consumer
8   gains protection by asking the question "What is the real cost of this
9   loan to me?" In deciding whether to charge items, the consumer must
10   determine if it is less expensive to pay cash. Yes, knowing the cost
11   of credit contributes to using it wisely.

273

Rule No. 18

Another type of dependent clause is the **adjective clause.** Like the appositive, it can be either essential (restrictive) or nonessential (nonrestrictive). Although nonessential clauses are certainly not limited to adjective clauses, these are the ones that generally give students the most trouble.

An essential clause _____ require commas.
        (will/will not)

A nonessential clause _____ require commas.
        (will/will not)

274

In punctuating essential and nonessential adjective clauses, treat them the same way you do appositives. The only difference between an appositive and an adjective clause is that the latter will have a subject and a verb and will be introduced by a relative pronoun such as *who, that, which, whose,* etc.

275

Which sentence below has a nonessential adjective clause? _____

(A/B/Both/Neither)

A. The Nile, a river in Egypt, is the longest river in the world.
B. The Amazon, which is a river that flows through Brazil, is the second longest river in the world.

276

Look closely at the adjective clauses in brackets; then answer the question that follows:

A. The American people, [who are willing to take risks in order to work for themselves], are said to be entrepreneurial.
B. People [who are willing to take risks in order to work for themselves] are said to be entrepreneurial.

Why does Sentence A have commas around the adjective clause, whereas Sentence B does not? _____

_____

277

Adjective clauses are dependent clauses, of course, in that they cannot stand alone. Like appositives, they may be either essential (restrictive) or nonessential (nonrestrictive). Use commas to set off a <u>nonrestrictive</u> adjective clause.

Ex.: 1. **Students who understood the frame preceding this one are doing well.**
     2. **Kinuyo Kimura, who understood the frame preceding this one, is doing well.**

The first example above is _____ in order to identify which students. In
                                    (essential/nonessential)
the second example the adjective clause is _____ because it follows a
                                                    (essential/nonessential)
proper noun.

278

Underline the adjective clauses in the following sentences:

A. Families whose income is below a certain standard are said to be living below the poverty line.
B. A time deposit, which is also called a certificate of deposit or a CD, requires the money be left on deposit for a specified period of time.

Circle the letter of the sentence below that contains an essential (restrictive) clause:

A. Inflation_ which hurts elderly people the worst_ "eats up" savings.
B. The purpose of Social Security is to provide income for workers_ who are retired or disabled.

279 ▶

Punctuate the sentence that has a nonessential (nonrestrictive) clause in it:

A. Students who major in business will take more of their course work in international studies.
B. This study which often covers several years helps the agent learn the principles of life insurance.
C. An individual who has only a small investment to make would likely benefit more by investing in no-load mutual funds.

280 ▶

Following each of the sentences below, write whether the clauses are essential (restrictive) or nonessential (nonrestrictive):

A. Jaymont Properties_ which acquires and manages properties with funds from European sources_ bought a block of office towers in downtown Dallas. _____
B. The company_ which understands the importance of name recognition in advertising_ will survive the international test of the 1990s. _____

281 ▶

Punctuate these sentences:

A. In a market economy the individual who has free choice directs business production by his or her demand through purchases.
B. In a market economy individuals who have the most dollar votes are the one who likewise influence production the most.

282 ▶

A nonrestrictive clause is not needed to identify the noun or pronoun it modifies. To test a phrase, omit it and see whether the meaning of the sentence is affected. If the phrase or clause identifies <u>which one</u>, commas cannot be used.

Circle the letters of the sentences containing nonrestrictive clauses below:

A. A worker_ who makes $3.50 an hour_ is being paid below minimum wage.
B. The program_ which is carried by 128 stations in 19 states_ broke into the Top 50 last week.
C. Insurance_ which means sharing the risks_ is the cornerstone of one's estate.
D. My insurance_ that I carry on my pickup truck_ comes due in the fall.

283 ▶

In the numbered blanks following the sentences below, state whether the clauses at each numbered point are essential (restrictive) or nonessential (nonrestrictive):

284

A. Dividends[1] which are part of the profit shareholders receive[2] are important to people[3] who live on fixed incomes.

B. An individual retirement account[4] which is known as an IRA[5] is important to Herman[6] who has no company retirement benefits.

1 & 2 _____   4 & 5 _____
3 _____   6 _____

285

Circle the numbers where a comma would be required in the preceding frame.

1   2   3   4   5   6

286

No response is required for this frame. Read the following paragraph carefully.

One of the most common problems of using commas is that of <u>overpunctuation</u>. When students aren't sure whether a comma should be used or not, they usually put one in. Commas should be used <u>only</u> if there is a need for them. Commas are oftentimes optional, but they are used mostly to assist the reader in grasping the meaning of the content. Certain rules exist to help a writer decide where commas are usually required to help prevent misunderstanding. Don't fall into the trap of <u>overpunctuation</u>.

287

Is the following sentence punctuated correctly? _____
(Yes/No)

In international trade each country has its own form of money, which complicates the process of buying and selling among countries.

Why is the sentence above correctly or incorrectly punctuated? _____

_____

288

Should the following sentence be punctuated with commas at either of the points indicated?

_____
(Yes/No)

A credit union is a group of people_ who agree to pool their money and make low-cost loans available to individuals_ who are members.

Why is the sentence above correctly or incorrectly punctuated? _____

_____

Like the conjunction *and* (discussed in Unit 2), the relative pronouns *who, which,* and *that* likewise tend to elicit overpunctuation.

Circle the letter of the sentence below that conveys Larry's dislike for rude people:

    A. Larry can't stand people, who are rude.

    B. Larry can't stand people who are rude.

289

Now, circle the letter of the sentence in the preceding frame which conveys the meaning that Larry doesn't like all people because people in general are rude:

    A or B

290

As you read each sentence below, delete the adjective clause in brackets. Which sentence is still complete in meaning without the clause? _____
                              (A/B)

    A. According to the author [who wrote *In Search of Excellence*] most successful companies compete by improving quality rather than by lowering prices.

    B. According to Thomas J. Peters [who wrote *In Search of Excellence*] most successful companies compete by improving quality rather than by lowering prices.

291

Which sentence in the preceding frame should <u>not</u> have commas around the adjective clause?
_____

    (A/B/Both/Neither)

292

Punctuate the sentence that needs a comma:

    A. Taxes which are deducted from one's paycheck are our way of sharing in the great achievements of society.

    B. Taxes which are levied by the state are regulated by the state legislature.

293

Punctuate these sentences:

    A. Applications that are received before September 29 will be processed first.

    B. Applications which are time-consuming are sometimes filled out during a job interview.

    C. Applications that are received before September 29 1993 will be processed first.

294

Cross out and insert commas as necessary:

295

A. Our plant manager who is French by birth, outlined a new procedure, that would eliminate excess motion.

B. Construction workers, who don't work sometimes for several weeks at a time, have a strong union.

C. The plan, which was passed last week by the stockholders, should be the one management accepts.

296

No response is required for this frame. Please read the following information:

Adjective clauses obviously are not the only phrases that can be essential or nonessential. In addition to parentheticals, appositives, and adjective clauses, other essential and nonessential clauses are *verbal modifiers, adverbial clauses, contrasts,* etc.

Ex.: 1. **Verbal modifier: Armando Reyes, _realizing_ his mistake, corrected the error at once.**

2. **Adverbial clause: Armando Reyes, _when_ he realized his mistake, corrected the error at once.**

3. **Contrast: Armando Reyes, _not_ Scott Plummer, found the mistake.**

297

All nonessential phrases are punctuated the same way: Commas are placed around them if they are _not_ needed to complete the identity of the words they modify.

Circle the letter of the sentence(s) below containing an underlined phrase that is nonessential, thus requiring commas:

A. The statute of limitations guidelines _not the file clerks_ shall determine whether or not a document can be destroyed.

B. Restrictions on output or production _whether by labor or management_ tend to reduce the standard of living.

298

Punctuate these sentences _if_ they contain a nonessential phrase:

A. The term beneficiary indicates the person to whom the insurance will be paid in case of death of the insured.

B. Money management which is synonymous with careful planning and spending is a problem for most of us.

299

Insert all necessary commas in the following:

A. The saver who buys Series E government bonds is making a secure investment.

B. Property and liability insurance is possible through small payments collected from many people to pay unexpected losses that may occur to any one of the policyholders.

Insert commas:

A. J. B. Rhine who founded the once world-famous parapsychology laboratory at Duke University was a protégé of the psychologist William MacDougall.

B. An embargo a government action which stops completely the importing and exporting of products is sometimes used.

300 ▶

For the last time:

A nonessential phrase (will/will not) have commas around it. Nonessentials (are/are not) needed for the meaning to be complete and do not help to _____ which one. Sometimes an essential or nonessential phrase is a matter of _____. The critical question making a phrase nonessential is "Can the phrase be _____ without impairing the meaning of the sentence?"

301 ▶

Watch for review as you punctuate these sentences:

A. In December REI acquired Mohawk Data Sciences Ltd a Canadian company for $103 (10 point 3) million in cash and 200000 shares of REI common stock.

B. Working capital which is another term used in business is money that is spent for daily operation such as wages materials and other expenses

302 ▶

Punctuate:

A. Incidentally corporation profits which create more jobs for more people by stimulating economic growth are used to expand the business

B. Nevertheless a report released Monday by the Commodities Trading Commission which regulates futures markets exonerated trading from any role in the crash

303 ▶

This completes Section 4. You are about two-thirds of the way through the program at this point. The hardest part is definitely behind you. Restrictive (essential) and nonrestrictive (nonessential) clauses are always very difficult for students.

Take the section test for Section 4. After you have inserted all marks of punctuation, turn the page and check yourself carefully. The final page is for your review; it lists all the items in the test by number and tells you in what frame(s) you can review the item. Do not skip over this checking process, for it will help you clear up any difficulties before going on to Section 5.

February 17 19__

Whirlwind Travel Service
Attention: K H Henderson Agent
121 W Hickory Blvd
Springfield MA 01115-2393

Ladies and Gentlemen

A year ago on Sunday January 11 I flew to New Orleans Louisiana for an NBA convention(E) Upon arrival at the departure gate Gate 41 at 7:25 pm I discovered that I had lost my ticket which had fallen out of a book that I was carrying(E) I panicked as you can imagine because the plane was leaving at 7:55 pm(E)

The ticket agent who was on duty at the gate told me that she could not issue a boarding pass to me without a ticket(E) She told me to try to find the ticket in the main lobby the area where it apparently had been lost(E) Therefore I headed down the corridor went back through security and raced to the main lobby(E) Well no ticket could be found anywhere(E)

Because the lines were too long the main ticket counter was of no help(E) One of the porters who worked in the lobby asked if he could be of any assistance(E) I explained to him that I had lost my ticket and that my plane would be leaving for New Orleans Louisiana in ten minutes or less(E)

Ms Christine Carter who was the supervisor of ticketing overheard the commotion and told me that if I wanted to make Flight #217 I would have to purchase another one-way ticket which would cost $_____ (two hundred seventy-nine dollars)(E) Although I had only $_____ (seventy-five dollars) in cash I did have my charge card which had been sent to me only three days earlier(E) Thank goodness(E) When I finally got another ticket received my boarding pass and entered the plane the pilot was announcing that everyone including all flight attendants should be seated for takeoff(E) Wow I made it but just barely(E)

Now one year later I am requesting a refund for the lost ticket(E) If the original ticket was never turned in that means it was unused in which case a refund is due(E) Would you please contact my office in Holyoke Massachusetts by Wednesday March 10(E) I have been waiting as you advised over a year ago for the opportunity to apply for this refund(E)

Sincerely

R. Thornton Meyers Vice President
East Coast Branch, Continental U S

February 17,[1] 19___

Whirlwind Travel[2] Service[3]
Attention: K. H. Henderson,[4] Agent
121 W.[5] Hickory Blvd.[6]
Springfield,[7] MA[8] 01115-2393

Ladies and Gentlemen:[9]

A year[10] ago on Sunday,[10] January 11,[11] I flew to New Orleans,[12] Louisiana,[13] for an NBA[14] convention. Upon arrival at the departure gate,[15] Gate 41,[16] at 7:25[17] p. m.,[18][19][20] I discovered that[21] I had lost my ticket,[21] which had fallen out of a book[22] that I was carrying.[23][24] I panicked,[24] as you can imagine,[25] because the plane was leaving at 7:55 p. m.[26][27][28]!

The ticket agent[29] who was on duty at the gate[30] told me that she could not issue a boarding pass to me without a ticket.[31] She told me to try to find the ticket in the main lobby,[32] the area where it apparently had been lost.[33] Therefore,[34] I headed down the corridor,[35] went back through security,[36*] and raced to the main lobby.[37] Well,[38] no ticket could be found anywhere.[39]

Because the lines were too long,[40] the main ticket counter was of no help.[41] One of the porters[42] who worked in the lobby[43] asked if he could be of any assistance.[44] I explained to him[45] that I had lost my ticket[46] and that my plane would be leaving for New Orleans, Louisiana,[47] in ten minutes[48] or less.[49][50]

Ms.[51] Christine Carter,[52] who was the supervisor of ticketing,[53] overheard the commotion[54] and told me that[55] if I wanted to make Flight #217,[56] I would have to purchase another one-way ticket,[57] which would cost $279.[58][59] Although I had only $75[60] in cash,[61] I did have my charge card,[62] which had been sent to me only three days earlier.[63] Thank goodness![64] When I finally got another ticket,[65] received my boarding pass,[66*] and entered the plane,[67] the pilot was announcing that everyone,[68] including all flight attendants,[69] should be seated for takeoff.[70] Wow![71] I made it,[72] but just barely![73]

Now,[74] one year later,[75] I am requesting a refund for the lost ticket.[76] If the original ticket was never turned in,[77] that means it was unused,[78*] in which case[79] a refund is due.[80] Would you please contact my office in Holyoke,[81] Massachusetts,[82] by Wednesday,[83] March 10.[84] I have been waiting,[85] as you advised over a year ago,[86] for the opportunity to apply for this refund.[87]

Sincerely,[88]

R.[89] Thornton Meyers,[90] Vice President
East Coast Branch,[91] Continental U. S.[92]

REVIEW SHEET

If you missed Number	See Frame Number	Practice Sentence
1	100, 97	_____
2	15	_____
3	15	_____
4	119, 115	_____
5	15	_____
6	15	_____
7	103	_____
8	107, 110	_____
9	140	_____
10	97	_____
11	97	_____
12	103	_____
13	103, 105	_____
14	17	_____
15	2	_____
16	245, 248	_____
17	245, 248	_____
18	15	_____
19	15	_____
20	157, 150	_____
21	275, 274	_____
22	283, 275	_____
23	2	_____
24	201, 203	_____
25	201, 203	_____
26	15	_____
27	15	_____
28	6, 19	_____
29	283	_____
30	283	_____
31	2	_____

If you missed Number	See Frame Number	Practice Sentence
32	245, 248	_____
33	2	_____
34	226, 228	_____
35	57	_____
36	57, 59	_____
37	2	_____
38	215	_____
39	2	_____
40	162, 157	_____
41	2	_____
42	283	_____
43	283	_____
44	2	_____
45	289, 286	_____
46	64, 69	_____
47	103	_____
48	103, 105	_____
49	64, 286	_____
50	2	_____
51	15, 19	_____
52	277, 283	_____
53	277, 283	_____
54	64, 286	_____
55	286	_____
56	162, 157	_____
57	275, 283	_____
58	27	_____
59	2	_____
60	27	_____
61	162	_____
62	283	_____
63	2	_____
64	7	_____
65	57	_____
66	57, 59	_____

If you missed Number	See Frame Number	Practice Sentence
67	162, 157	_____
68	251, 245	_____
69	251	_____
70	2	_____
71	7	_____
72	296	_____
73	6	_____
74	245, 248	_____
75	245, 248	_____
76	2	_____
77	157	_____
78	296	_____
79	286	_____
80	2	_____
81	103	_____
82	103, 105	_____
83	97	_____
84	32	_____
85	201, 203	_____
86	201, 203	_____
87	2	_____
88	140	_____
89	15	_____
90	119	_____
91	15, 16	_____
92	15, 16	_____

appositive
New Orleans
Raymond Harrison
fiduciary of the estate

245

A. (the path that a product travels from producer to consumer)
B. (whole life)

246

follow

247

A. brother, Steven,
B. population, over 66 million Americans,

248

Tennessee, touched by eight states,   Elvis, the king of rock and roll.

249

A. The <u>Consumer Product Safety Commission</u>, created in 1972,
B. The <u>FTC</u>, established in 1915,

250

A. A filing fee, usually under $10,
B. Tax money, especially money spent on national defense,
C. seals of approval, particularly the Good Housekeeping Seal,

251

Tariffs, <u>sometimes known as customs duties,</u>
imports, <u>usually the latter.</u>

252

Ⓐ & Ⓑ (Both appositives could be removed without changing the meaning.)

253

A. The Truth in Lending Bill, passed by Congress in 1968,
B. Information processing, a term which includes all communication technologies,

254

Ⓒ.

255

identifies

256

Ⓑ John Kenneth Galbraith answers the question <u>which</u> economist?

257

which one?   (or which friend?)
essential

258

Ⓑ Reports, a reference work available in most libraries,   (In Sentence A, *Best's Insurance Reports* identifies <u>which</u> reference book, therefore requiring no comma.)

259

A. Aggregate demand, the total demand of all people for goods and services produced by an economy,

B. No commas.   (Ted Kennedy identifies <u>which</u> senator.)

260

No commas. The appositive is essential to the complete meaning of the sentence.

261

should not
should

262

Chopin, the greatest of all Polish composers, wrote his composition_ Polonaise in G Minor_ when he was only seven years old.   (The second appositive is essential to identify <u>which</u> composition.)

263

more than one
which one

264

This
the appositive *owned by us* identifies which partnership you are talking about.

265

proper nouns
nonessential

266 ▶

A. National debt, the amount of money owed by the federal government,
B. Optional, depending upon meaning.   (If Linda has only one sister, commas would be used around the appositive Katherine; if Linda has several sisters, no commas would be used around Katherine to identify which sister.)
C. Proprietorship, a form of business in which one individual owns the entire business,

267 ▶

(B.)
3M
, which we talked about in class last Friday,

268 ▶

A. Disposable income, the money that is left over after taxes,
B. bond, a liability to a corporation,

269 ▶

A. Gross national product, the value of the total quantities of all goods and services produced,
B. No commas. (In this case the appositive *regulated by governments* identifies which monopolies. Some people might argue that all monopolies are regulated by governments, in which case commas would be used.)

270 ▶

271

judgment

272

___✔___ B.

273

Line 1—credit (It renames *term.* It is essential to identify which term, so no commas are used.)
Line 3—, a service for which a consumer pays,
Line 5—, especially one that could cause bankruptcy,
Lines 8 and 9— "What is the real cost of this loan to me?"   (This appositive identifies what question you are speaking of; therefore, it is not set off by commas.)

If you completed this frame correctly, pat yourself on the back; you really do understand appositives.

274

will not
will

B.

275 ►

The adjective clause in Sentence A merely gives additional information about the American people. The adjective clause in Sentence B actually identifies which people you are referring to.

276 ►

essential
nonessential

277 ►

A. whose income is below a certain standard
B. , which is also called a certificate of deposit or a CD,

278 ►

279

Ⓑ.

280

B. This study, which often covers several years, helps the agent learn the principles of life insurance.   (This study is specific, and the adjective clause explains rather than identifies.)

281

A. nonessential   (The adjective clause does not identify; it merely provides added information about Jaymont Properties.)
B. essential   (Not all companies will survive; only those who understand the importance of name recognition will.)

282

A. individual, who has free choice,   (The adjective clause is not intended to identify.)
B. None (The adjective clause is needed to identify which individuals.)

283

A. No commas   (The clause is needed to identify what worker makes below minimum wage.)
Ⓑ. Commas   (The phrase does not help to identify the program.)
Ⓒ. Commas   (The clause gives added information, but does not identify.)
D. No commas   (Since you probably have more than one insurance policy, the clause is needed to identify which insurance.)

1 & 2—nonessential
3—essential
4 & 5—nonessential
6—nonessential

284 ▶

  3 ④ ⑤ ⑥

285 ▶

No response is needed.

286 ▶

Yes   The adjective clause (beginning with the word <u>which</u>) is nonessential. It does not identify the word money in any way; therefore, it can be removed without impairing the complete meaning.

287 ▶

No   Both adjective clauses (beginning with the word <u>who</u>) are essential. They identify <u>which</u> people and <u>which</u> individuals. A credit union is not just any group of people, and loans aren't made to just any individuals.

288 ▶

289

Ⓑ

290

Ⓐ

291

B

292

A. (The adjective clause is needed to identify which author. A comma <u>should</u> be placed after the word *Excellence* because of the long introductory expression.)

293

A. Taxes, which are deducted from one's paycheck, . . .   (The phrase merely gives added information.)

294

A. No commas   (The clause tells which applications.)
B. Applications, which are time-consuming,   (The clause does not identify which applications.)
C. September 29, 1993, (Although the clause is essential, commas are always placed around the year in a three-part date.)

A. manager, who is French by birth, . . . procedure,   (The clause is interesting information. If you left the comma before the word *that,* reread Frames 286 and 289.)
B. The sentence is correct.   (The clause is nonessential.)
C. Probably no commas, depending on your meaning.   (If the clause is needed to identify which plan, no commas would be used. If the clause is meant to give further information, commas would be used.)

295

No response is needed.

296

(A.) & (B.)   Both are nonessential.   (If you read Frame 296 carefully and understood its meaning, you should have had no trouble answering this frame correctly.)

297

A. No commas around beneficiary   (This word is essential to identify which term.)
B. Money management, which is synonymous with careful planning and spending,   (The phrase is not essential to the meaning; therefore, commas should be placed around the clause.)

298

A. None   (The adjective clause is essential.)
B. None   (Although long, this sentence does not contain any nonessential clauses or phrases.)

299

300

A. J. B. Rhine, who founded the once world-famous parapsychology laboratory at Duke University,

B. An embargo, a government action which stops completely the importing and exporting of products,

301

will

are not

identify

judgment (or opinion)

omitted (or left out)

302

A. In December REI acquired Mohawk Data Sciences, Ltd., a Canadian company, for $10.3 million in cash and 200,000 shares of REI common stock.

B. Working capital, which is another term used in business, is money that is spent for daily operation such as wages, materials, and other expenses.

303

A. Incidentally, corporation profits, which create more jobs for more people by stimulating economic growth, are used to expand the business.

B. Nevertheless, a report released Monday by the Commodities Trading Commission, which regulates futures markets, exonerated trading from any role in the crash.

Section 5

304

Up to this point the punctuation you have learned has been commas for dependent clauses. Now we will turn our attention to the *independent* or *main clause*, which is a clause that is complete in meaning and can stand alone.

1   2
[If customers can take their business elsewhere], [sellers must compete for sales].

Which part of the above sentence is the independent clause? _____

(1/2)

305

A **dependent clause** contains a subject and a verb but is not a complete thought in itself; an **independent clause** will always contain a subject and a verb and is a complete thought in itself.

Place the adjective (dependent) clause below in brackets and underline the independent clause:

Because expansions are longer than recessions, GNP in the United States has generally been increasing.

306

Underline the subject once and the verb twice in the independent clause below:

Social Security, which is a mandatory form of insurance, gives us a way of providing for our old age during the years of greatest income.

307

A main clause and an independent clause are the same thing. Whereas the *dependent clause* depends on the main clause for its meaning, a *main* (independent) *clause* is complete in meaning.

Underline the independent clause twice and the dependent clause once in the following sentence:

Instead of exploring new investment opportunities, most people stick with investments they know and have made before.

308

Circle the letter of the sentence below which contains only an independent clause:

A. A rate of exchange is the value of the money of one country expressed in terms of the money of another country.
B. Thus, as prices increase, wages also tend to increase.

309

An independent clause will contain both a _____ and a _____ and will express a complete _____.

Rule No. 19

Quite frequently two main clauses will occur in the same sentence. The two separate thoughts will usually be very similar in meaning (related) and may be connected by the simple conjunctions *and*, *but*, *so*, *or*, *nor*, and *for*. When this happens, a comma is used to separate the two clauses.

> Ex.: **[Wage rates above the minimum required by law are determined by supply and demand]**, *but* **[many conditions may affect wages].**

Underline the subject once and the verb twice in both independent clauses above.

▸ **310**

Does this sentence contain two independent clauses (two separate thoughts both containing a subject and a verb)? _____
(Yes/No)

The top 200 largest corporations in the U.S. are responsible for about 70 percent of all business conducted in this country.

▸ **311**

How many <u>independent</u> clauses does this sentence contain?

The dollar's steady decline, which leaves many consumers muttering about steadily rising import prices, might help create 730,000 jobs this year.

▸ **312**

The comma used with a simple (coordinating) conjunction between two independent clauses is always placed <u>before</u> the conjunction.

> Right: Liquidity may be important, <u>but</u> such investments typically do not create high rates of return on one's investments.
>
> Wrong: Stockholders are owners <u>but</u>, bondholders are creditors.

Given two independent clauses connected by one of the following simple conjunctions, which one would be punctuated correctly? (Circle the letter of the correct answer.)

A. so,
B. , and,
C. , but

▸ **313**

Punctuate the two independent clauses in both these sentences:

A. The U.S. has only about 5.4 percent of the world's population <u>and</u> yet it produces about 25 percent of the total goods and services.

B. Common stock allows stockholders to vote <u>but</u> preferred stock usually has no voting privileges.

▸ **314**

315

Is the comma correct between the two clauses in the following sentence? _____
(Yes/No)

Competition is one means of protection for the consumer, for it helps to keep down prices.

Analysis: 1. Are there two independent thoughts?
2. Do these thoughts both contain a subject and a verb?
3. Is there a simple conjunction (*and*, *but*, *for*, etc.) connecting the two clauses?

If you can answer *yes* to all three questions, a comma will be required.

316

If a subject does not appear in the second clause, that clause cannot stand alone; thus, no comma will be used before the conjunction if the subject is missing, unless there is another reason for the comma.

Wrong: A stock certificate contains the name of the owner, and lists the number of shares owned.

Right: A stock certificate contains the name of the owner, and <u>it</u> also lists the number of shares owned.

In the above examples the reason the first example is wrong is that: (Circle the letter of the correct answer.)

A. there is no conjunction between the two clauses.
B. the first clause is not independent.
C. the comma should go after the conjunction rather than before.
D. the part following the conjunction is not an independent clause because the subject is missing.

317

Are both clauses in the following sentence independent? _____ Why? _____
(Yes/No)

_____

The market posted its third record drop in a week <u>and</u> is in the midst of a panic.

318

Is the following sentence punctuated correctly? _____
(Yes/No)

Let your gains ride, but be sure to cut your losses before they become too great.

Circle the letter of the sentence that can be punctuated before the conjunction:

    A. Consumers normally purchase all the goods necessary to satisfy their basic needs <u>and</u> many have extra income left over for leisure and recreation.

    B. Consumers normally purchase all the goods necessary to satisfy their basic needs <u>and</u> at the same time have income left over.

319 ▶

Punctuate these sentences:

    A. Employers are required to withhold a portion of employees' wages and send these withholdings to the IRS.

    B. Some experts say that the lag time between the change in money supply and its effect on the economy is unpredictable.

    C. Term insurance is often referred to as pure insurance because it provides protection only.

If you completed this frame without making an error, you may advance to Frame 323.

320 ▶

Circle the letter of the sentence that contains two independent clauses:

    A. Better Business Bureaus are nonprofit organizations, and they provide information to consumers about local businesses.

    B. Economic activity is any act that is concerned with satisfying human wants and needs for goods and services through production, distribution, and consumption.

321 ▶

Punctuate if the clauses are independent:

    A. Be cautious with penny stocks and try to avoid short selling in unstable economic times.

    B. A cooperative is a business that is owned by its members and its customers are its members.

322 ▶

Does the sentence below contain two independent clauses? _____
                                        (Yes/No)

A contract specifies [that one person or group will do certain things] and [that another person or group will do other things in return].

323 ▶

Again, as the preceding frame illustrates, be careful not to insert a comma every time you see a conjunction. Conjunctions connect many things besides two independent clauses.

324

Punctuate the following sentences <u>if</u> necessary:

A. The government is the country's largest employer and also its biggest borrower.
B. A person's life insurance savings and investment program should be planned in conjunction with that person's last will and testament.

325

Although the following sentence does not contain two independent clauses, a comma is required before the *and*. Why? _____

Two of the better known consumer information services are the Consumers' Research, Inc., and Consumers' Union of the United States.

326

How many <u>main</u> clauses does each of these sentences contain? _____
(One/Two/Three)

A. Keeping a flawless credit rating is important, for merchants exchange information about their customers' pay records through an agency called a credit bureau.
B. The balance of trade is favorable if the aggregate value of exports exceeds imports and unfavorable if the value of imports exceeds exports.

327

Watch for review as you cross out any unnecessary commas in the following sentences:

A. The Truth in Lending Bill, which was passed by Congress, in 1968, requires, that the lender state both the monthly, and the annual percentage rate and, that the exact cost of the loan be spelled out to the borrower.
B. Everyone appears to be preoccupied with money matters to some degree, but, a key difference is, that higher income people are more concerned with investments while the poor, are thinking about how to pay their bills.

328

Watch for review as you cross out and insert commas as needed:

A. For example, a Japanese company may provide its employees with, free housing meals, and, medical care.
B. The 11th annual salary survey from Hewitt Associates, in Lincolnshire, Illinois which queried 1274 U S companies, revealed that, the average salaried worker received a 48 (4 decimal 8) percent raise, last year.

168

Insert all necessary punctuation:

A. Farms building sites minerals forests and water are all natural resources which are needed in production

B. Once the customers' needs are identified producers must decide what resources to use and in what quantities to make a product that satisfies those needs

329

Insert punctuation:

A. The government for example has taken over much of our railway system and has partially paid for its operation through Amtrak

B. A technological change would generally increase productivity and in turn this would lower the cost of production

330

A comma is required in most independent clauses connected by *and*, *but*, *for*, etc. However, when the clauses are very short and closely related, the comma may be omitted—unless confusion would result.

Ex.: 1. I walked but Curtis rode.
     2. Bette played and I sang.

Glenda is shy but Paul isn't.

Would the sentence above need a comma? _____
                                    (Yes/No)

331

Circle the letter of the sentence from which the comma before the simple conjunction could be omitted:

A. There are laws against discrimination in the workplace, but the EEOC receives thousands of complaints every year.

B. I agree, and you should too.

332

Punctuate these sentences if necessary:

A. Donna played guard and Celeste played center.

B. We all worked and we all played.

333

334

If there is a chance two short clauses will be misread, definitely insert a comma.

Ex.: **The driver hit the wall and the car behind him swerved out of control.**

The driver did not hit the car behind him as well as the wall, so put a comma before the _____ in the above example.

335

Circle the letter of the sentence that would need a comma because of possible confusion if omitted:

A. Water is a natural resource but air is free.
B. Spot ate the scraps and his master ate steak.

336

Punctuate the following sentences:

A. Interest is taxed and deferred savings isn't.
B. The bank encourages borrowers and savers are usually overlooked.

337

Rule No. 20

Another good practice in business writing is to put a semicolon before the simple coordinating conjunction (*and*, *but*, *so*, *for*, *or*, etc.) when either of the two independent clauses already contains a comma.

OK: Of course, if the price is set too low, operating costs will not be covered, and the supplier may be forced to go out of business.

BETTER: Sales taxes apply to virtually all purchases; but many states exempt a few items such as clothing, restaurant meals, public utility services, food, and medicine.

As shown above, either a _____ or a _____ is acceptable between two independent clauses when either of the clauses already _____; however, a _____ is preferable.

338

Since this program is following the best practices of good business writing, you will want to use the <u>semicolon</u> before the conjunction between two independent clauses that are already punctuated with commas.

Many people enjoy helping others through volunteer work, but in the final analysis, most people work to earn an income.

Is the above sentence correct according to the best business punctuation standards? _____
(Yes/No)

Circle the letter of the sentence that would need a semicolon at the point indicated:

  A. Most people want to acquire wealth_ and they want to do it by owning property.
  B. Most people want to acquire wealth_ and they want to own more land, buildings, and personal possessions.

339 ▶

Punctuate these sentences:

  A. Talk about the car of the future and most designers envision dazzling dashboard computer displays.
  B. Apple Computer Inc., slashed the price of its Mac Plus and their board of directors argued for even further price cuts.

340 ▶

Commas in amounts of money or apostrophes in possessive words are not considered to be internal punctuation.

  Ex.: This country's franchises are popular in fast-food chains, but few franchises exist in high-quality restaurants.

In the above example the apostrophe and hyphens (are/are not) considered as internal punctuation; therefore, a (comma/semicolon) should be used before the conjunction.

341 ▶

Punctuate these sentences using either a comma or a semicolon as needed:

  A. When competition is perfect there are many buyers and sellers and no one in the market is able to influence the price unfairly.
  B. The level of "real" wages varies with the nation's productivity so a $1,000 increase will be worth $1,000 only if the worker's productivity also increases.

342 ▶

According to the *Wall Street Journal*, only one in twenty corporate women travels for business; but, in contrast, among male executives the rate is one in three.

  Is the sentence above punctuated correctly? _____ Why? _____
  (Yes/No)

343 ▶

_____

You do realize, of course, that both clauses must be <u>independent</u> before either a comma or a semicolon may be used.

Punctuate the following sentences:

344

A. A family should have adequate life insurance and a sizable "emergency" fund before investing in securities.

B. It is wise to be careful of all spending and to know what happens to the money that is spent.

C. After the stock market crash of 1929 and during the Great Depression of the following decade one out of four persons was unemployed and national income plunged to all-time low levels.

No response is required for this frame. Read the material that follows.

You know that:

345

1. a comma is used to connect two independent clauses at the simple conjunction (*and*, *but*, *for*, etc.).

2. no comma is used if the sentence contains a binary rather than two indpendent clauses.

3 a comma is optional after two very short clauses connected by one of the simple conjunctions. However, the comma must be used if confusion could result.

4. a semicolon is used at the simple conjunction if punctuation exists in either of the independent clauses.

Punctuate the sentence(s) that need(s) a semicolon at the points indicated:

346

A. Generally speaking, credit unions offer the lowest interest rates_ and consumer finance companies have the highest.

B. Some economists have projected that Japan, the economic wonder of the latter half of the 20th century, will become the world's largest economy by the Year 2010_ and will surpass West Germany's GNP by twice.

Punctuate these sentences:

347

A. Capital is the amount of wealth owned by a person or a company and it usually takes the form of savings.

B. Goods that are free, like the air we breathe have great value because people cannot live without them but the free air does not have economic value because it ordinarily cannot be bought or sold.

Punctuate:

A. While an investment should offer a good rate of return it should also be reasonably easy to get when needed.

B. Charge accounts and credit cards should be used as a convenience, not as a means of buying before having the means to pay and people who overextend themselves financially usually pay twice.

348

Read this frame rapidly. No overt response is required.

A comma is the weakest mark of punctuation.
A semicolon is halfway between a comma and a period.
A period indicates a strong pause.
An exclamation point calls for an abrupt halt.

Punctuation marks are used to guide the reader smoothly and safely through a piece of writing. If there is a chance the reader might stumble, the writer should smooth the rough spots. Most punctuation is logical if you just stop and think about it. Much of modern-day punctuation is optional and is left up to the judgment of the writer. Don't get upset when the rules aren't "set in stone." One of the beautiful features of the English language is that it is flexible.

349

Rule No. 21

A comma is placed between two independent clauses connected by the simple coordinating conjunctions *and*, *but*, *for*, *so*, etc. But what happens when the coordinating conjunction is left out? The clauses are still independent and closely enough related that a comma is insufficient; yet a period is too strong. What's left? Of course, the <u>semicolon</u>.

Use a semicolon between two closely related independent clauses when the conjunction has been omitted.

Ex.: Direct taxes cannot be passed on to others; indirect taxes can be.

A _____ is used between two independent clauses when the clauses are connected by a conjunction; a _____ is used when the conjunction is missing.

350

Circle the letter of the sentence which contains two independent clauses:

A. Business is our principal means of satisfying human wants_ it produces whatever the consumer demands.

B. Business is our principal means of satisfying human wants_ and produces whatever the consumer demands.

351

352

In the preceding frame would Sentence A or Sentence B require a semicolon? _____
What punctuation should be used in the other sentence? _____

353

Punctuate this sentence:

An investment club is a small group of people who organize to invest their money and who meet regularly to decide how much is needed from members to buy stocks in even lots, thus avoiding higher brokerage fees.

354

Circle the letter of the sentence that is correctly punctuated:

A. Samuel rents his home Sandra owns hers.
B. Samuel rents his home; Sandra owns hers.
C. Samuel rents his home, Sandra owns hers.

355

Underline the subjects once and the verbs twice in the sentence below:

Some feel that most people can handle small losses and favor insuring against only major or catastrophic losses.

Does the sentence above need additional punctuation? _____ Why? _____
                                                        (Yes/No)

_____

356

The semicolon takes the place of the _____ and the simple _____ between two independent clauses when the connective is missing.

357

Punctuate this sentence:

Property damage insurance protects the other person's car collision insurance protects your own car.

358

On the lines provided, tell what is wrong with the punctuation in this sentence:

Banks are operated as private businesses, they are the centers of financial transactions for both individuals and corporations.

_____

_____

Is this sentence punctuated correctly? _____
(Yes/No)

Insurance attempts to spread losses among many people; and it protects the insured against extreme losses.

359

Circle the letter of the sentence which has the punctuation correctly inserted:

A. Phoenix, Arizona is expected to have one of the largest population increases between now and the year 2000, the population of New York City is expected to decline.
B. Phoenix, Arizona, is expected to have one of the largest population increases between now and the year 2000; the population of New York City is expected to decline.

360

Punctuate these sentences:

A. High-volume production of a commodity tends to lower prices low volume tends to raise prices however.
B. During prolonged high inflationary periods judicious borrowing is more appealing cash savings lose money because inflation eats up more than the interest earned.

361

Why does the following sentence need a semicolon at the points indicated?

About 70 percent of the United States businesses have a single owner_ about 10 percent are partnerships_ about 20 percent are corporations.

Because _____ .

362

Is the following sentence punctuated correctly? _____
(Yes/No)

Personal checks may not be accepted for some important payments but, certified checks or cashier's checks may be used instead.

363

Is the following sentence correctly punctuated? _____
(Yes/No)

Money is rapidly disappearing as a medium of exchange; and, without a doubt, the day will come when few actual dollars will change hands.

364

365

Punctuate the sentences below:

A. One should pay most bills by check a canceled check can serve as a receipt.
B. Prices in a market economy are influenced by supply and demand but certain monopolies can threaten the workings of a pricing system if left unchecked.

366

Try punctuating these sentences:

A. Recognizing opportunity isn't enough taking action is what separates entrepreneurs from innovative people who accomplish nothing.
B. Government exists for the people and when a government ceases to serve the people, the people should change the government.

367

The following sentence should have both semicolons and commas. Insert them where they are needed:

When an economic system is in the growth part of the cycle it is said to be in a period of expansion but when it is in the downward part of the cycle it is in recession.

368

Quickly flip back and reread Frame 226. Pay particularly close attention to the use of the semicolon in Example 2.

369

Frequently, two independent clauses are joined by a connective other than a simple conjunction (*and*, *but*, *so*, *for*, etc.). Some of the more common transitional expressions are words such as *however*, *nevertheless*, *therefore*, *consequently*, *moreover*, etc. Multiple-word transitional expressions are phrases such as *of course*, *that is*, *such as*, *for example*, etc.

The function of a conjunction is to _____ a thought to a preceding one. The function of _____ words is to move the sentence into the next part.

No response is required for this frame. Read the following material:

So far, you have learned that a semicolon is used between two independent clauses when:

1. either of the two clauses already contains commas.
2. the conjunction has been omitted between the clauses.

A third use of the semicolon is this:

Use a semicolon between two independent clauses when they are connected by such words as *however*, *therefore*, *consequently*, and *nevertheless*. When such expressions are meant to link a clause with a preceding thought, a <u>semicolon</u> is used before the conjunction and a <u>comma</u> after the conjunction.

370

Note the following examples of two independent clauses connected by one of the longer conjunctions:

Ex.: **1. In Marx's utopia no one would own the means of production; therefore, no one could exploit his or her co-workers.**
   2. Dividends by corporations are usually paid in cash; however, a stockholder might be offered a choice of cash or additional shares of the company's stock.

As shown above, a _____ is used before the conjunction to separate the two independent clauses with a _____ following the conjunction.

371

Although no comma follows the simple conjunction (*and*, *but*, etc.), a comma <u>is</u> used after the longer coordinating conjunctions.

Circle the letter of the correctly punctuated sentence:

A. If you are employed, your social security tax is taken out of your salary moreover; your employer must pay an equal amount.
B. The dividend must be declared by the company's board of directors; moreover, the rate of dividend is stated as a certain number of dollars or cents on each share.

372

Circle the places where the following sentence is punctuated incorrectly:

Competition has cut company sales for the past five years, therefore 2200 workers will be laid off.

373

Insert the punctuation mark(s) needed to make the following sentence correct:

Competition has cut company sales for the past five years therefore 2200 workers will be laid off.

374

375

Remember, long conjunctions or transitional words can be used to connect two independent clauses:

Ex.: 1. **In a free enterprise system, earning and spending decisions are decentralized; moreover, decisions are made by individuals.**

2. **In a free enterprise system, earning and spending decisions are decentralized; for example, individuals make the decisions about what is produced by their aggregate purchases.**

As shown in the above examples, a semicolon is used before the longer _____ and/or _____ words. A _____ is used after such connectors.

376

Which sentence is punctuated correctly? _____
(A/B/Both/Neither)

A. Advertising costs are reflected in the selling price of a product or service; therefore, the consumer ultimately pays for advertising.
B. Advertising costs are reflected in the selling price of a product or service; that is, the consumer ultimately pays for advertising.

377

Correct the following sentence:

As a nation we cannot satisfy all our economic wants, therefore, we must make choices.

378

Circle the letter of the correctly punctuated sentence below:

A. Americans want neither inflation nor deflation; therefore we strive for few ups and downs, which is economic stability.
B. Americans want neither inflation nor deflation, therefore, we strive for few ups and downs, which is economic stability.
C. Americans want neither inflation nor deflation; therefore, we strive for few ups and downs, which is economic stability.
D. Americans want neither inflation nor deflation, therefore we strive for few ups and downs which is economic stability.

Once again, don't confuse a conjunction with a parenthetical expression. Words such as *therefore*, *however*, *of course*, and *in fact* can be used as either. The way to tell the difference is to ask yourself this question: "Does the expression connect two independent clauses, or does it interrupt a single thought?"

▶ **379**

If the word *however* interrupts a thought, a _____ will be used both before and after. If the word *however* connects two independent clauses, a _____ comes before the conjunction and a _____ goes after the conjunction.

Circle the letter of the sentence that contains a conjunction:

▶ **380**

   A. A business run by one person however is called a sole proprietorship.
   B. Almost all large firms are incorporated indeed they have to be in order to raise the vast sums of money they need.

Watch for review as you cross out all unnecessary punctuation in the following sentence:

▶ **381**

For example, if money is scarce, and rates are high, it is difficult for families to buy, or build a new home; consequently, fewer home starts are made by builders; and there are fewer jobs for workers.

Watch for review as you change the punctuation in these sentences:

▶ **382**

   A. I will never give up, we will win.
   B. Gross profit is the difference between the cost and the selling price; but, net profit is gross profit minus operating expenses.

Punctuate the following sentences taking into account everything you have learned about commas and semicolons:

▶ **383**

   A. Owners of common stock usually have voting rights but they have the lowest priority in claiming dividends bondholders and preferred stockholders come first.
   B. The functions of money are to serve as a common medium of exchange and to act as a common measure of value.
   C. Almost everything you own is an economic good for example the clothes that you are wearing or the breakfast you had this morning are economic goods

Read carefully and punctuate:

 A. For a high school student graduating means an extra $5000 per year in earning power college students who finish college earn $8000 a year more than those who don't get a degree

 B. When demand falls and businesses lower production unemployment begins to rise this phase of the business cycle known as a recession typically follows long periods of sustained growth

You might like to know that you have just completed the most difficult portion of this text. There are a few additional marks of punctuation that you will need to put the finishing touches on your skill, but definitely the hardest part has been in the last three sections.

Take the section test for Section 5, following the directions given in Section 1. After you have inserted all marks of punctuation, turn the page and check yourself carefully. The final page is for your review; it lists all the items in the test by number and tells you in what frame(s) you can review the item. Do not skip over this checking process, for it will help you clear up any difficulties before moving on to Section 6.

MEMO REPORT

TO: Dr John D Palmer Sr

FROM: Esther Beck Consultant *E.B.*

DATE: June 9 19___

SUBJ: Speed-Rite an alphabetic shorthand system

Thank you so much for your letter and the very helpful materials that you sent for my study on Speed-Rite an alphabetic shorthand system(E) My article which has just been accepted for publication by U S News and World Report will appear in the September 15 19___ issue(E)

Well when you say that most of the current literature is of the "I like it because" variety you are absolutely correct(E) As I read the few articles chapters and promotional literature that are available I try to keep in mind that even though everyone seems to be enthusiastic about Speed-Rite those who try it and who don't succeed seldom write about it(E) In fact I have not found one negation any-where(E) No not one user however poor they might believe the system to be has written unfavorably about Speed-Rite(E)

Probably the only way an individual can find out for sure about the system and its potential is to conduct an experimental study(E) This would involve sending out questionnaires contacting schools who are presently teaching Speed-Rite in their curriculums questioning business executives about their attitudes toward the system checking out those persons who are now using it on the job etc(E) Obvi-ously this would be a tremendous challenge for any one person to accept however this is what needs to be done(E)

You asked to see a copy of the results when my current research project was finished I am pleased to be able to enclose a photocopy(E) If I may rationalize however I am disappointed in not being able to find out more(E) As I stated though this topic could easily be a three-year research effort(E) I like the conclu-sions but because of the importance of the subject I wish more could be drawn from the data(E)

Any comments that you would like to make would be appreciated Mr Palmer and do keep the paper for as long as you like(E) Remember everything is copyrighted so none of the material can be duplicated for any other use yet except your own reading(E) When you are finished would you please send it on to W Lafayette In-diana and have Mrs Wang Ho the director of Manpower Inc review it critically. Once again your interest in this endeavor has been extremely valuable(E)

Enclosure

MEMO REPORT

TO: Dr.[1] John D.[2] Palmer,[3] Sr.[4]

FROM: Esther Beck,[5] Consultant *E B.*

DATE: June 9,[6] 19__

SUBJ: Speed-Rite,[7] an alphabetic shorthand system

Thank you so much for your letter[8] and the very helpful materials[9] that you sent for my study on Speed-Rite,[10] an alphabetic shorthand system.[11] My article,[12] which has just been accepted for publication by U.[13]S.[14] News and World Report,[15] will appear in the September 15,[16] 19__,[17] issue.[18]

Well,[19] when you say that most of the current literature is of the[20] "I like it be-cause" variety,[21] you are absolutely correct![22*] As I read the few articles,[23] chapters,[24] and promotional literature[25] that are available,[26] I try to keep in mind[27] that even though everyone seems to be enthusiastic about Speed-Rite,[28] those who try it[29] and who don't succeed[30] seldom write about it.[31] In fact,[32] I have not found one negation[33] anywhere.[34] No,[35] not one user,[36] however poor they might believe the system to be,[37] has written unfavorably about Speed-Rite.[38]

Probably[39] the only way an individual can find out[40] for sure[41] about the system[42] and its potential[43] is to[44] conduct an experimental study. This would involve[45] sending out questionnaires,[46] contacting schools[47] who are presently teaching Speed-Rite in their curriculums,[48] questioning business executives about their attitudes toward the system,[49] checking out those persons[50] who are now using it on the job,[51] etc.[52] Obviously,[53] this would be a tremendous challenge for any one person to accept;[54] however,[55] this is what needs to be done.[56]

You asked to see a copy of the results[57] when my current research project was finished;[58] I am pleased to be able to enclose a photocopy.[59] If I may rationalize,[60] however,[61] I am disappointed in not being able to find out more.[62] As I stated,[63] though,[64] this topic could easily be a three-year research effort.[65] I like the conclusions;[66] but[67] because of the importance of the subject,[68] I wish more could be drawn from the data.[69]

Any comments[70] that you would like to make[71] would be appreciated,[72] Mr.[73] Palmer;[74] and[75] do keep the paper for as long as you like.[76] Remember,[77] everything[80] is copyrighted;[78] so[79] none[81] of the material can be duplicated for any other use yet except your own reading.[82] When you are finished,[83] would you please send it on to W.[84] Lafayette,[85] Indiana,[86] and have Mrs.[87] Wang Ho,[88] the director of Manpower, Inc.,[89][90] review it critically.[91] Once again,[92] your interest in this endeavor has been extremely valuable.[93]

Enclosure

SECTION 5
REVIEW SHEET

If you missed Number	See Frame Number	Practice Sentence
1	15	
2	15	
3	125	
4	15	
5	115	
6	245, 248	
7	100	
8	64, 72	
9	275, 277, 283	
10	245, 248	
11	2	
12	277, 283	
13	15	
14	15	
15	277, 283	
16	90	
17	90, 97	
18	2	
19	215	
20	286	
21	157, 163, 168	
22	6	
23	57	
24	57, 59	
25	277, 283	
26	163	
27	277, 283	
28	163	
29	64, 72	
30	277, 283	
31	2	

If you missed Number	See Frame Number	Practice Sentence
32	201, 207	_____
33	286	_____
34	2	_____
35	215	_____
36	379	_____
37	201, 379	_____
38	2	_____
39	286	_____
40	286	_____
41	286	_____
42	64, 72	_____
43	286, 196	_____
44	2	_____
45	196, 286	_____
46	57	_____
47	275, 283	_____
48	57	_____
49	57	_____
50	275, 283	_____
51	73	_____
52	15, 18	_____
53	201, 203	_____
54	369, 370	_____
55	372	_____
56	2	_____
57	163	_____
58	350	_____
59	2	_____
60	201, 203	_____
61	201, 163	_____
62	2	_____
63	201, 203	_____
64	201, 163	_____
65	2	_____

If you missed Number	See Frame Number	Practice Sentence
66	337, 338	_____
67	337, 372	_____
68	163	_____
69	2	_____
70	286	_____
71	286, 196	_____
72	221	_____
73	15	_____
74	337, 338	_____
75	310, 313	_____
76	2	_____
77	201	_____
78	337, 338	_____
79	337, 313	_____
80	286	_____
81	2	_____
82	163	_____
83	15	_____
84	103	_____
85	103, 105	_____
86	15	_____
87	266	_____
88	129	_____
89	15	_____
90	129, 266	_____
91	32	_____
92	201, 203	_____
93	2	_____

2

304 ▶

[Because expansions are longer than recessions], <u>GNP in the United States has generally been increasing</u>.

305 ▶

<u>Social Security</u>   <u>gives</u>

306 ▶

<u>Instead of exploring new investment opportunities</u>, <u>most people stick with investments they know and have made before.</u>

307 ▶

Ⓐ

308 ▶

subject
verb
thought

309 ▶

Wage rates   are determined
conditions   may affect

310

No   (The sentence ends with several prepositional phrases.)

311

One   (The commas set off a nonrestrictive dependent clause, which you learned about in the preceding unit.)

312

C.

313

314

A. population, and   (The comma always goes <u>before</u> the simple conjunction.)
B. vote, but   (A comma is not placed after the simple conjunction.)

Yes   (The sentence meets the criteria.)

315 ▶

Ⓓ

316 ▶

No   The second clause has no subject; therefore, it cannot stand alone.   (**NOTE:** Even if you think the subject is obvious, if it is not repeated or stated, the clause will not be independent. The only subject that can be implied is *you*.)

317 ▶

Yes   (*You* is the understood or implied subject in both independent clauses. Please reread Instructional Frame 316 and Feedback Frame 317 if you missed this item.)

318 ▶

319

Ⓐ (In Sentence B the second clause contains no subject.)

320

None should be punctuated.

321

Ⓐ (Although long, Sentence B contains a binary and a series. See Frames 62–64 for review if you missed it.)

322

A. stocks, and   (*You* is the understood subject of both clauses.)
B. members, and   (Both clauses are independent because they contain a subject and a verb, and they are connected by a simple conjunction.)

323 No

A. None   (The sentence contains a binary. See Frame 64 if you have forgotten.)
B. insurance, savings, and investment program   (The sentence contains a series. Did you remember the comma before the conjunction connecting the last element? See Frame 57 or 59 if you have forgotten.)

324

Because commas are placed around the word *Inc.*

325

A. Two
B. One

326

A. The Truth in Lending Bill, which was passed by Congress/ in 1968, requires/ that the lender state both the monthly/ and the annual percentage rate and/ that the exact cost of the loan be spelled out to the borrower.
B. Everyone appears to be preoccupied with money matters to some degree, but/ a key difference is/ that higher income people are more concerned with investments while the poor/ are thinking about how to pay their bills.

327

A. For example, a Japanese company may provide its employees with/ free housing, meals, and/ medical care.
B. The 11th annual salary survey from Hewitt Associates/ in Lincolnshire, Illinois, which queried 1,274 U.S. companies, revealed that/ the average salaried worker received a 4.8 percent raise/ last year.

328

329

A. Farms, building sites, minerals, forests, and water are all natural resources which are needed in production.

B. Once the customers' needs are identified, producers must decide what resources to use and in what quantities to make a product that satisfies those needs.

330

A. The government, for example, has taken over much of our railway system and has partially paid for its operation through Amtrak.

B. A technological change would generally increase productivity, and in turn this would lower the cost of production.

331

No   (A comma is not required, but it is not incorrect to insert one. Most authorities leave it out. The trend is toward as few commas as possible.)

332

B.   (The comma may be omitted because the clauses are short and closely related.)

333

Neither needs a comma before the simple conjunction. Both clauses are short and are very closely related.

and   (simple conjunction)

334 ▶

Ⓑ (At first it sounds as if Spot ate <u>both</u> the scraps and his master.)

335 ▶

A. No comma   (The closely related clauses are short, and no confusion would likely occur if the comma before the simple conjunction is left out.)
B. borrowers,   (Otherwise, *borrowers* and *savers* might at first be read together.)

336 ▶

comma
semicolon
has a comma
semicolon

337 ▶

338 ▶

No (There should be a semicolon after the word *work* because of the comma in the second clause.)

339   Ⓑ (A semicolon is needed at the simple conjunction because the second independent clause already contains commas.)

340

A. future,
B. Apple Computer, Inc.,   Plus; and

341

are not
comma

342

A. perfect,   sellers;
B. productivity,

343

Yes.   If one or the other of the independent clauses already has a comma (in this case they both do), a semicolon rather than a comma is preferable at the simple conjunction.

A. No punctuation   (The sentence contains a binary.)
B. No punctuation   (The conjunction connects the binary to be careful . . . . <u>and</u> to know.)
C. decade,   unemployed;   (The first *and* connects a binary. The hyphenated word does not affect the choice of a comma or a semicolon, but the comma after the introductory phrases makes a semicolon preferable between the two independent clauses.)

▶ 344

No response is needed.

▶ 345

A. rates; and
B. No semicolon or comma   (The last clause does not contain a subject and therefore cannot stand alone.)

▶ 346

A. company, and
B. breathe,   them;

▶ 347

195

348

A. return,
B. means to pay; and

349

No response is needed.

350

comma
semicolon

351

Ⓐ.

Sentence A
None   (The subject in the second clause is missing in Sentence B.)

▶ **352** ▶

No further punctuation is needed.

▶ **353** ▶

B) (The clauses in all three sentences contain a subject and a verb. Since there is no conjunction, a semicolon is required.)

▶ **354** ▶

<u>Some</u> <u>feel</u>   people <u>can handle</u> . . . and <u>favor</u>
No.   The clause after the simple conjunction does not have a subject. Such constructions are known as binaries, which have been discussed and reviewed.

▶ **355** ▶

comma
conjunction

▶ **356** ▶

other person's car; (Do you see that if a simple conjunction were used before the word *collision*, a comma would be all that is necessary?)

▶ **357** ▶

▶ **358** ▶

A semicolon should be used after the word *businesses*.   (This common punctuation error is referred to as a run-on sentence. A **run-on sentence** erroneously connects two main clauses with a comma when a conjunction or a semicolon is needed.

359 No (The simple conjunction between two independent clauses requires only a comma <u>unless</u> there is punctuation in one of the clauses.)

360 B. (In Sentence A, remember to put a comma after the state as well as after the city. Also, to avoid a run-on sentence, two independent clauses with no conjunction require a semi-colon rather than a comma.)

361 A. prices; low . . . prices, however. (Did you remember the comma needed to set off the parenthetical expression *however*?)
B. periods, appealing;

362 the conjunctions are missing

363 No (If you said yes, go back and reread Frame 313; read it carefully.)

364 Yes (Since the second clause already contains commas, a semicolon is preferred before the simple conjunction. Note that the parenthetical expression directly following the con-junction is the only time a comma is placed after a simple conjunction.)

A. check;
B. demand,

365

A. enough;
B. Government exists for the people;   (A semicolon is used because of the comma in the second clause.)

366

growth part of the cycle,   period of expansion;   downward part of the cycle,

367

No written response is needed.

368

369

connect   (join, link)
transitional

No response is needed.

370

semicolon
comma

371

Ⓑ.

372

(years,)   (therefore)   (2200)

373

374

years;   therefore,   2,200

conjunctions
transitional
comma

375 ▶

Both

376 ▶

wants;

377 ▶

Ⓒ.

378 ▶

379

comma
semicolon
comma

380

(B) (The first sentence contains a parenthetical expression. Remember, an independent clause must follow the conjunction.)

381

scarce/,   buy/,   (All other punctuation marks are needed.)

382

A. up; (A comma makes this a run-on sentence.)
B. price, but/, (Only longer connectives require a semicolon followed by a comma. Use a comma with two independent clauses connected by a simple conjunction.)

383

A. rights, but . . . dividends;
B. No further punctuation is needed.
C. good; for example, . . . goods. (Did you put a comma after the word *wearing*? If so please go back to Frame 64 to read about binaries and Frame 286 to read about the problem of overpunctuating.)

A. student, (optional) $5,000   power; $8,000   degree.
B. production,   rise;   cycle,   known as a recession,   growth.

384

Section 6

BASIC RULES

No. 22 Apostrophe	Contractions
No. 23 Apostrophe	Possessives
No. 24 Quotation marks	Quoted material, slang, technical terms, and words used for emphasis

SUPPLEMENTARY USAGE

Contractions and informality

Forming singular possessives

Forming plural possessives

Forming plural possessives of plural nouns not ending in <u>s</u>

Keeping a complete (real) word before the apostrophe

Forming a possessive with an <u>of</u> phrase

Making proper nouns possessive

Possessives vs. pronouns

Possessives vs. plurals

Making lowercase letters plural by using an apostrophe

Distinguishing pronoun contractions and possessive pronouns

Using <u>your/you're</u> and <u>its/it's</u> correctly

Rule No. 22

Use an apostrophe to indicate contractions of words. The apostrophe indicates that two words have been fused into one, and it should be placed at the point where the letter(s) have been omitted.

Right: Are not   Aren't (the o is missing)
Wrong: Are not   Are'nt

On the line beside each contraction, write the words that the contraction represents:

can't _____   shouldn't _____

isn't _____   wasn't _____

haven't _____   don't _____

If the apostrophe is inserted where letters or numbers have been omitted, where would you place an apostrophe in these contractions? Supply the apostrophe for each of these words:

A. doesnt   (does not)
B. couldnt   (could not)
C. Id   (I would)
D. theyve   (they have)
E. Class of 99 (1999)

What letters have been omitted in these contractions?

A. couldn't   _____
B. let's   _____
C. we'll   _____
D. who's   _____
E. o'clock   _____

Circle the contractions which have the apostrophe in the correct place:

did'nt   were'nt   would'nt   are'nt

Contractions tend to be informal. Although contractions are used in business writing, their excessive use should be avoided.

> Ex.: 1. **Although <u>you've</u> been a good customer of ours for many years, we <u>haven't</u> provided all the services <u>we've</u> wanted to mainly because <u>it's</u> been impossible to contact every customer monthly.**

Circle a letter below to correctly complete the following:

For business writing, the example above probably is

A. very formal.
B. neither formal nor informal.
C. too informal.

389 ▶

Indicate what letters have been omitted in the four underscored contractions in the preceding frame:

_____   _____

_____   _____

390 ▶

Is the following statement true or false?

All contractions should be avoided in business writing. _____

(True/False)

391 ▶

Rule No. 23

Apostrophes are also used to show the possessive form of nouns. Possessives, as you probably recall from previous English courses, indicate ownership.

> Ex.: **When a <u>family's</u> income is small, some life insurance is needed to protect the dependents in the event the primary wage earner should die.**

In the above example, to whom does the income belong? <u>the</u>_____

392 ▶

To form the singular possessive (SP), usually add the apostrophe and s ('s) to the word.

> Ex.: **Rodney<u>'s</u> younger brother had a doctor<u>'s</u> appointment.**

Make these nouns singular possessive:

A. the secretary_ _ knowledge
B. Father_ _ loving care
C. a pilot_ _ dream

393 ▶

To form the plural possessive (PP) of plural nouns already ending in s, merely add the apostrophe after the s (s').

394

> Ex.: 1. authors novels   = authors' novels
> 2. the tenants rights = tenants' rights

Make these plural nouns plural possessive (PP):

- A. the lawyers alliance (many lawyers)
- B. dogs barking (several dogs)
- C. the customers requests (numerous customers)

395

Insert the apostrophe in the following phrases:

- A. the editors corrections (one editor)
- B. the editors corrections (two or more editors)
- C. the editors correction (three editors making the same correction)

396

Circle the letter(s) of the phrases that have the apostrophe correctly inserted:

- A. an agent's region
- B. the senators' constituency
- C. five teacher's plans

When the plural noun does <u>not</u> end in s, the plural possessive (PP) is formed by adding an apostrophe and s ('s).

397

> Ex.: 1. mice = mice's tails
> 2. women = women's hats

Make these plural nouns PP:

- A. men_ _ suits
- B. children_ _ toys
- C. deer_ _ antlers

Have you noticed that when a plural is made by changing the word form rather than by adding s (the normal plural), both the singular possessive and plural possessive are made by adding an apostrophe and an s ('s)?

Ex.: 1. man   men   man's   men's
     2. child   children   child's   children's
     3. alumnus   alumni   alumnus's   alumni's

Is the following underscored word SP or PP? _____

     the <u>editors-in-chief's</u> responsibilities

398 ►

How would the responsibilities of one editor-in-chief be written?
the _____ responsibilities

399 ►

What are the singular possessive and plural possessive of the word <u>ox</u>?

     SP _____
     PP _____

400 ►

One important principle to remember about possessives is that a <u>real</u> (legitimate) word must <u>precede</u> the apostrophe. For example, the word *wives* would have to be wives' in the PP. If you wrote *wive's,* you can see that there is no such word as *wive.*

Form the SP and PP of each of these words:

		SP	*PP*
A.	calf calves	_____	_____
B.	goose geese	_____	_____
C.	sheep sheep	_____	_____
D.	thief thieves	_____	_____

401 ►

Write whether the word is SP or PP in the blank provided:

     A. the senators' remarks _____
     B. our neighbors' flowers _____
     C. Glady's new dress _____

402 ►

Write the singular, plural, SP, and PP for the following words:

	Singular	*Plural*	*SP*	*PP*
Ex.:	mother	mothers	mother's	mothers'
1.	_____	gentlemen	_____	_____
2.	lady	_____	_____	_____
3.	_____	attorneys general	_____	_____
4.	coach	_____	_____	_____

403

404

Why is the apostrophe used incorrectly in each of these last names?

Bower's   Burn's   Byer's   Lyon's   Morale's

Because _____

_____

A possessive can be reversed to form an <u>of</u> phrase.

Ex.: Fido's bone = the bone of Fido

If you aren't sure a noun is possessive, try making the word an <u>of</u> phrase.

405

Substitute an <u>of</u> phrase for the following possessive nouns: (No written response is required; you may simply think the answer to yourself.)

A. The <u>country's</u> trade deficit was beginning to affect the economy adversely.
B. An <u>engineer's</u> career advancement will depend upon that <u>engineer's</u> education.

406

Change the underlined phrase below to a possessive noun: _____

Federal Reserve banks are <u>banks of bankers</u> and cannot be used by the public.

An apostrophe plus an <u>of</u> phrase are unnecessary and, therefore, redundant.

Wrong: The goal <u>of</u> Arnold's
Right: The goal of Arnold
Right: Arnold's goal

407

Circle the letter(s) of the sentences below that are correct:

A. The messages of the boss's were all by phone.
B. The message's of the boss's were all by phone.
C. The boss's messages were all by phone.
D. The messages of the boss were all by phone.

If you have difficulty deciding whether the possessive should be 's or s', think of the singular and plural forms of the word and then decide. You know that:

1. a SP will be 's.
2. a PP will be s' when the plural ends in s.
3. a PP will be 's when the plural does not end in s (changes form from the singular to the plural).
4. a real word must precede the apostrophe.

What is the PP of the word *chief*?
What is the PP of the word *family*?

408 ▶

Using the four points given in the preceding frame as a guide, go back to Frame 403 and re-work any that you missed the first time.

409 ▶

Punctuate these sentences with apostrophes:

A. Most peoples benefits from workers compensation will be tied directly to wages.   (several workers)
B. Lets look at a typical example of how competitors advertising often gives false information about a products safety.   (many competitors)

410 ▶

Punctuate the following:

A. A cashiers check is a check that a bank draws on its own in-house funds.
B. *Bests Insurance Reports* can be found in most libraries reference section.

411 ▶

In making a person's name or a proper noun possessive, use an 's. Some authorities say that if the name ends in s, ss, or x making it difficult to pronounce, an apostrophe following the last letter is sufficient.

Ex.: 1. **Morris**   = **Morris's**
     2. **Gates**   = **Gates's or Gates'**
     3. **Cendejas** = **Cendejas's or Cendejas'**

Use an apostrophe to show two ways you could write this phrase:

Metzelaars old Mercedes.

412 ▶

Once again, a real word must precede the apostrophe. Students sometimes get careless and cut off the last part of a word or a name with an apostrophe.

> Ex.: 1. **Craig Parkins'** NOT **Craig Parkin's**
> 2. **Robert Stevens'** NOT **Robert Steven's**

413

Which sentence below has the apostrophe placed correctly? _____
(A/B/Both/Neither)

A. Simmon's Oldsmobile (Simmons)
B. Keye's Print Shop (Keyes)

Another common error that writers make is using an apostrophe in a pronoun to show possession. Remember, an apostrophe is used only with a noun to show possession.

> Right: Ours and yours
> Wrong: Her's and your's

414

Is the apostrophe needed in the following sentence? _____
(Yes/No)

Their's was the only boat on the lake at 5:30 a.m.

Circle the letters of the phrases below that have the apostrophe used correctly:

A. Buds' jacket
B. Davis's file
C. Wendy Corliss's sister
D. Alan Grove's driveway (Groves)

415

Punctuate the following sentences: (Watch for both contractions and possessives.)

A. Two cant live as cheaply as one because last years statistics show that it cost 40 percent more to maintain a couples standard of living than a single persons standard.
B. The United States national average for saving by individuals is 5 percent; Japans average, by contrast, isnt as high as it once was, but its still around 20 percent.

416

Don't get carried away with the apostrophe. Be sure that the word possesses something before making it possessive. Another very common error made by unskilled writers is using an apostrophe to form simple plurals.

417

Is the following sentence punctuated correctly? _____
(Yes/No)

Many small investor's are unable to buy a variety of stock's and bond's.

Correct the sample sentence in the preceding frame and list the plural words.

_____   _____   _____

418 ▶

Circle the letter of the sentence(s) below which contain(s) possessive words:

A. The state attorney general's office or a local tenants' group are good sources of information.
B. Some person's might value job mobility more than owning a home.

419 ▶

In the following sentence all nouns ending in s have the s underscored. Decide whether the word is plural or possessive, and insert an apostrophe for any possessive nouns:

In many case<u>s</u> the law requires seller<u>s</u> to provide minimum standard<u>s</u> of quality even if no actual promise<u>s</u> are made at the time<u>s</u> of the sale<u>s</u>.

420 ▶

Plurals of *lowercase letters* are made by using an apostrophe. Capital letters and figures no longer use an apostrophe to form plurals.

Ex.: 1. Your m's look very much like your n's.
2. Her Ks and Rs are easy to read.
3. The 7s, 3s, and 9s are mistotaled.

Punctuate this sentence:

Letters at the end of the alphabet—us, ws, ys, etc.—are hard to write in shorthand.

421 ▶

Another common error is the confusion of pronoun contractions with possessive pronouns:

Contractions	*Pronouns*
it's	its
they're	their
who's	whose
you're	your

Underscore the correct word in parentheses:

According to the above, (its/it's) is a pronoun and (its/it's) is a contraction; you're is a (pronoun/contraction) and your is a (pronoun/contraction).

422 ▶

423

Circle the letter of the sentence in which the pronoun is used correctly:

A. Your the one who decides what financial security you will achieve in you're life.
B. Whose portfolio is over $25,000?
C. Their only human, too.
D. The stock market was it's own worst enemy.

424

Of the pronouns listed in Frame 423, *your* and *its* are probably the most frequently missed by students.

Ex.: 1. Wrong: <u>Your</u> certainly welcome to join us.
     Right: <u>You're</u> certainly welcome to join us.
  2. Wrong: As <u>it's</u> cities grew larger, <u>it's</u> industrial base expanded.
     Right: As <u>its</u> cities grew larger, <u>its</u> industrial base expanded.

In the above examples, the first one requires a (pronoun/contraction); the second one requires a (pronoun/contraction). (Underscore the answers.)

425

Learn to distinguish between <u>its</u> as a pronoun and <u>it's</u> as a contraction. Since personal pronouns such as your<u>s</u>, her<u>s</u>, and their<u>s</u> do not use an apostrophe, it<u>s</u> as a pronoun likewise does not use an apostrophe.

Underline the correct usage in parentheses below:

(Its/It's) fun to try to locate all (its/it's) hidden meanings.

426

Circle the letter of the sentence below which uses <u>its/it's</u> correctly:

A. Its the judgment of most economists that next year will be the beginning of a recession.
B. Its a healthy sign for all three indicators to be up.

427

Anytime you aren't sure about whether to write *its* or *it's,* substitute the words *it is.* If you can use these words, you will want to write _____
                                (its/it's)

428

Insert and delete apostrophes in the following sentences:

A. Your's is the only job besides Sammie Roger's that Id like to have.
B. Its best feature is it's flexibility in switching from fixed to variable.

Insert and delete apostrophes as needed:

A. Audrey McWilliam's horse beat our's in the race, but its too bad your's couldnt have placed. (McWilliams)

B. At three oclock lets plan to meet to study, for my two D's are'nt helping this semesters average.

429

Circle the letter of the sentence below that is punctuated correctly:

A. You're t's and 2's are easy to read; her's are not.

B. Vasquez's hardware store will have it's annual spring sale, and your invited.

C. Its not always easy to set forth your investment goals.

D. Their the ones who's fortunes were made in this countries' real estate boom of the 70's.

E. It's wise to seek counsel on your insurance decisions.

430

Correct each misuse of the apostrophe (underscored words) in the preceding frame.

A. _____

B. _____

C. _____

D. _____

E. _____

431

Circle the letter of the correctly punctuated sentence from the pair below:

A. Don't you see that the manufacturer's costs, as well as ours, are affected by style changes. (all manufacturers)

B. It's too bad you weren't able to hear the recital.

432

Which sentence is punctuated correctly?

A. Borrowing on ones life insurance policy isnt recommended since its easy not to pay back the amount youve borrowed.

B. A customers opinion of a firm can be greatly influenced by the appearance of its employees.

433

215

434

Circle the letter of the correctly punctuated sentence:

A. Summers advice was that auto insurance isnt a luxury; its a necessity. (Summers)
B. A budget will not spend one's money, but it'll help one spend for those things wanted most.

435

Correct all the errors in the A sentences in the last three frames:

Frame 432: _____
Frame 433: _____
Frame 434: _____

436

Punctuate the next few frames inserting any needed marks of punctuation: (Watch for review of all marks of punctuation.)

A. Sammons brother was here last week and he questioned the secretaries long coffee breaks. (all five secretaries)
B. Because the Fed is not a part of the Federal Government its not required to follow the Presidents orders

437

Watch for review of all punctuation as you punctuate these sentences:

A. Phillips Inc a seller of petroleum products isnt one of the worlds largest
B. Overall however a country tries to keep its trade in balance if it doesnt and it has no other way of making up the deficit its money will flow out of the countrys banks

438

Punctuate inserting all necessary marks of punctuation:

A. Lil Orbits Inc in Minneapolis Minnesota hired three sales representatives increasing its work force to 1025
B. In ones role as a consumer one must make decisions regarding spending borrowing saving and investing
C. Whether the family should carry disability insurance depends on the sick leave provisions of the wage earners job workers compensation provisions and other factors

Rule No. 24

No response is required for this frame. Please read the material that follows:

The use of the quotation marks is rather infrequent in business; nevertheless, it might be well to know that periods and commas are always placed <u>inside</u> the quotation marks regardless of how the quotes are used.

Use quotation marks to:

1. enclose the exact words of a speaker or a writer, or any <u>quoted material</u>.
2. set off <u>slang</u> expressions. (This tells the reader that you are aware the word is slang.)
3. set off <u>unusual</u> or <u>technical</u> words.
4. set off words intended to be <u>emphasized</u>.

439

Place quotation marks around the <u>quoted material</u> in the following sentences:

A. Langford, their attorney, made the statement, The creditors settled for 25 cents on the dollar.
B. Marx wrote: Capitalists are robbers who steal the fruits of the worker's toil.

440

What <u>slang</u> expressions below would you place in quotation marks?

A. Garbage in, garbage out is a well-known phrase in the computer field.
B. Catching that fly ball in the sun was really a fluke.
C. Driving at or below the speed limit will keep the fuzz off your tail.

441

Put quotation marks around the <u>technical</u> or <u>unusual</u> terms below:

A. Adam Smith's invisible hand is not a difficult idea.
B. Many countries use a floating exchange rate—the price that the nation's money can change (float) from one day to the next.
C. When revenue from a tax is specifically designated for some use, the tax revenue is said to be earmarked.

442

If you want to <u>emphasize</u> a word or a phrase, you may put quotes around it.

Ex.: Families should have an "emergency fund" of three to six times their monthly income.

Which words in the following sentences would you possibly want to emphasize?

A. Money is sometimes referred to as the oil that makes an economic system work more efficiently.
B. You will see supermarket ads for a great buy on orange juice, soft drinks, or eggs.
C. Monopoly comes from the Greek language and means single seller.

443

Place quotation marks around the words below that:

1. are direct quotes.
2. are slang.
3. you wish to emphasize.
4. are technical terms.

444

A. Decisions of what to produce, how much, and for whom are made by consumers who cast their dollar votes.
B. The dispute turned into a real brouhaha before the day was over.
C. Anything that is acceptable as money is called legal tender.
D. The classical version of inflation as stated by many economists is this: too much money chasing too few goods.

NOTE: Because the use of most quotation marks, except for a direct quotation, is strictly at the option of the writer, you will not be required to use them either in the section test for Section 6 or on the final examination. If anything other than a direct quotation is meant to be in quotes, the quotation marks will be supplied.

Take Section Test 6. It emphasizes the use of the apostrophe and has a review of other punctuation. In completing the section test, follow the directions given in Section 1. After you have inserted all marks of punctuation, turn the page and check yourself carefully. The final page is for your review; it lists all the items in the test by number and tells you in what frame(s) you can find the item. Do not skip over this checking process, for it will help you clear up any difficulties before beginning Section 7.

September 23 19___

Samson Skinner & Ponce Inc
Attention Ms Wanda Rhiney Chairperson
1409 S Hampton Dr
Hurst TX 76053

Ladies and Gentlemen

The economy is starting to resemble the hapless hostess who gives a dinner party but isnt successful in getting anybody to show up(E) Output grew at a 32 (three decimal point two) percent annual rate from January 1 19___ to April 1 19___ stated Wayne P Clarke(E) However (consumers/consumer's) held on to (their/they're) dollars and spent at a 28 (two decimal point eight) percent rate(E) Business capital investment fell almost as fast(E) When people arent buying how can the economy grow(E) It cant(E)

The outlook for 19___ is 75:25 odds for weak growth and 50:50 odds for no growth said Phylicia M Janvier chief economist at Shearson Inc(E) As businesses warehouses bulge with unsold goods (companies/company's) arent expected to fill (their/they're) new orders thus forcing (manufacturers/manufacturer's) to slash production(E) Nervous about Wall Street turmoil businesses will hold back on new investments, causing consumers to remain cautious because of slow growth in (their/they're) personal incomes(E)

Meanwhile interest (rates/rate's) are falling(E) Since May 10 19___ fixed mortgage rates have dropped from 107 (ten decimal point seven) to 102 (ten decimal point two) percent(E) If the Fed gets (its/it's) way interest rates will be pushed even lower to hold off a recession(E) Most private economists however expect the Fed to wield (its/it's) power very carefully(E) Any abrupt decision to cut rates warns John R Spencer of Gingles and Gingles Inc could create a gigantic chain reaction that could send the dollar plummeting thus pushing interest rates back up(E)

Tell everyone to make plans accordingly(E)

Sincerely

Herman R Paez Jr

lt

219

September 23, 19___

Samson, Skinner & Ponce, Inc.
Attention Ms. Wanda Rhiney, Chairperson
1409 S. Hampton Dr.
Hurst, TX 76053

Ladies and Gentlemen:

The economy is starting to resemble the hapless hostess who gives a dinner party but isn't successful in getting anybody to show up. "Output grew at a 3.2 percent annual rate from January 1, 19___, to April 1, 19___," stated Wayne P. Clarke. However, consumers held on to their dollars and spent at a 2.8 percent rate. Business capital investment fell almost as fast. When people aren't buying, how can the economy grow? It can't!

"The outlook for 19___ is 75:25 odds for weak growth and 50:50 odds for no growth," said Phylicia M. Janvier, chief economist at Shearson, Inc. As businesses' warehouses bulge with unsold goods, companies aren't expected to fill their new orders, thus forcing manufacturers to slash production. Nervous about Wall Street turmoil, businesses will hold back on new investments, causing consumers to remain cautious because of slow growth in their personal incomes.

Meanwhile, interest rates are falling. Since May 10, 19___, fixed mortgage rates have dropped from 10.7 to 10.2 percent. If the Fed gets its way, interest rates will be pushed even lower to hold off a recession. Most private economists, however, expect the Fed to wield its power very carefully. "Any abrupt decision to cut rates," warns John R. Spencer of Gingles and Gingles, Inc., "could create a gigantic chain reaction that could send the dollar plummeting, thus pushing interest rates back up."

Tell everyone to make plans accordingly.

Sincerely,

Herman R. Paez, Jr.

lt

*Punctuation optional

If you missed Number	See Frame Number	Practice Sentence
1	90, 100	
2	57	
3	129 (Feedback)	
4	129	
5	15	
6	15	
7	115, 116	
8	15	
9	15	
10	103	
11	107	
12	140	
13	274, 283	
14	316, 324	
15	385	
16	2	
17	439	
18	25	
19	286	
20	90	
21	90, 97	
22	90	
23	90, 97	
24	439, 440	
25	15	
26	2	
27	207, 226	
28	417, 418	
29	422, 430	
30	64, 316	
31	25	

If you missed Number	See Frame Number	Practice Sentence
32	2	
33	2	
34	385	
35	157, 162	
36	10	
37	385	
38	6	
39	439	
40	196	
41	316, 64	
42	286	
43	439	
44	440	
45	15	
46	245, 257	
47	129	
48	15, 18	
49	392, 394	
50	157, 162	
51	417	
52	385	
53	422	
54	274	
55	417	
56	2	
57	157	
58	163	
59	422	
60	2	
61	203, 204, 226	
62	417, 286	
63	2	
64	90	
65	90, 97	
66	25	

If you missed Number	See Frame Number	Practice Sentence
67	25	
68	2	
69	424, 425	
70	157, 162	
71	163, 286	
72	2	
73	201, 207	
74	201, 207	
75	424, 425	
76	2	
77	439	
78	439	
79	440	
80	15	
81	129	
82	15	
83	129	
84	439	
85	274, 283	
86	274	
87	2, 439	
88	439	
89	2	
90	136	
91	15	
92	125	
93	15	

cannot   should not
is not   was not
have not   do not

385

A. doesn't
B. couldn't
C. I'd
D. they've
E. Class of '99

386

A. o   (could not)
B. u   (let us)
C. wi   (we will)
D. i   (who is)
E. f the (of the clock)

387

None should be circled.

388

C.

389

390

ha (you <u>ha</u>ve)
o (have n<u>o</u>t)
ha (we <u>ha</u>ve)
ha (it <u>ha</u>s)

391

False

392

family

393

A. secretary<u>'s</u>
B. Father<u>'s</u>
C. pilot<u>'s</u>

A. lawyer<u>s</u>'
B. dog<u>s</u>'
C. customer<u>s</u>'

394

A. editor<u>'s</u>
B. editor<u>s</u>'
C. editor<u>s</u>'

395

(A.) (In Sentence B since two senators probably wouldn't have the same constituency, the word would be senator's; in Sentence C plural possessive would be shown by s'—teachers'.)

396

A. men's
B. children's
C. deer's

397

398

Plural Possessive (NOTE: The only reason we use an apostrophe after the s is to distinguish between the SP and PP form. If the word changes form from the singular to the plural— editor-in-chief to editors-in-chief, for example—there is no need to make this distinction with the apostrophe. Therefore, an apostrophe s ('s) is all that is needed for both SP and PP.)

399

editor-in-chief's

400

SP   ox's
PP   oxen's
(The word changes form from singular to plural; therefore, there is no need to distinguish with the 's and s'.)

401

A. calf's   calves'   (Although the word changes form in the plural, a real word must pre-cede the apostrophe. There is no such word as *calve*.)
B. goose's   geese's   (The word changes form from the singular to the plural, and both are legitimate words.)
C. sheep's   sheep's   (Since one is *sheep* and four are *sheep*, you cannot write the PP sheeps'—there is no such word as sheeps!)
D. thief's   thieves'   (Again, *thieve* is not a real word.)

402

A. PP
B. PP
C. Neither!   (Do you see that the part preceding the apostrophe is not the real word? The name is Gladys, not Glady; and the only way this word can be made possessive is by main-taining the whole word before the apostrophe: Gladys's or Gladys'.)

1.	gentleman	gentlemen	gentleman's	gentlemen's
2.	lady	ladies	lady's	ladies'
3.	attorney general	attorneys general	attorney general's	attorneys general's
4.	coach	coaches	coach's	coaches'

403

The whole word must precede the apostrophe. The names are Bowers, Burns, Byers, Lyons, and Morales. (Please reread Frame 401 if you didn't answer this frame correctly.)

404

A. The trade deficit <u>of the country</u> . . .
B. The career advancement <u>of an engineer</u> . . . the education <u>of that engineer</u>.

405

bankers' banks   (plural possessive, i.e., many bankers)

406

Ⓒ and Ⓓ

407

408

chiefs'
families'

409

See Feedback Frame 403.

410

A. people's   workers'
B. Let's   competitors'   product's

411

A. cashier's   (Its is not a contraction in this sentence.)
B. Best's   libraries'

412

Metzelaars's
Metzelaars'

Neither   (You cannot cut off the last part of a person's name with an apostrophe!)

413 ▶

No   (Pronouns are already possessive, therefore making an apostrophe redundant.)

414 ▶

Ⓑ   and   Ⓒ

415 ▶

A. can't   year's   couple's   person's
B. United States'   Japan's   isn't   it's

416 ▶

No!

417 ▶

231

418

investor<u>s</u>
stock<u>s</u>
bond<u>s</u>

419

Ⓐ.

420

All nouns are plural, thus requiring no apostrophe. An apostrophe indicates a contraction or a possessive word—and infrequently a plural. Please read on—the next frame explains.

421

u'<u>s</u>, w'<u>s</u>, y'<u>s</u>,

422

<u>its</u>
<u>it's</u>
<u>contraction</u>
<u>pronoun</u>

Ⓑ.

423 ▶

contraction
pronoun

424 ▶

It's
its

425 ▶

Neither.　(Both are contractions for the meaning *it is*. If you got this frame right, pat yourself on the back; if not, hang it there and keep working!)

426 ▶

it's

427 ▶

A.　Your's is the only job besides Sammie Roger's (Rogers' or Rogers's) that I'd like to have.
B.　Its best feature is it's flexibility in switching from fixed to variable.

428 ▶

429

A. Audrey McWilliam's' horse beat our's in the race, but it's too bad your's couldn't have placed.
B. At three o'clock let's plan to meet to study, for my two Ds aren't helping this semester's average.

430

(E.)

431

A. Your t's and 2s are easy to read; hers are not.
B. Vasquez's hardware store will have its annual spring sale, and you're invited.
C. It's not always easy to set forth your investment goals.
D. They're the ones whose fortunes were made in this country's real estate boom of the '70s.
E. Correct

432

(B.)

433

Neither A nor B is correct.   (customer's in Sentence B)

B.

▶ 434

Frame 432: manufacturers'
Frame 433: one's   isn't   it's   you've
Frame 434: Summers' (or Summers's)   isn't   it's

▶ 435

A. Sammons' (or Sammons's)   week,   secretaries'
B. Government,   it's   President's orders.

▶ 436

A. Phillips, Inc.,   products,   isn't   world's largest.
B. Overall, however,   balance;   doesn't   deficit,   country's banks.

▶ 437

A. Lil Orbits, Inc.,   Minneapolis, Minnesota,   representatives,   1,025.
B. one's   consumer,   spending, borrowing, saving, and investing.
C. earner's job,   workers' compensation provisions,   factors.

▶ 438

No response is needed.

◀ **439**

◀ **440**

A. Langford, their attorney, made the statement, "The creditors settled for 25 cents on the dollar."
B. Marx wrote: "Capitalists are robbers who steal the fruits of the worker's toil."

◀ **441**

A. "Garbage in, garbage out"
B. "fluke."
C. "the fuzz"

◀ **442**

A. "invisible hand"
B. "floating exchange rate"
C. "earmarked."

A. "oil"
B. "great buy"
C. "single seller."

◀ **443**

A. "dollar votes."
B. "brouhaha"
C. "legal tender."
D. "too much money chasing too few goods."
    NOTE: You may have chosen to punctuate a bit differently. If so your way may be equally acceptable.

444 ▶

Section 7

Rule No. 25

445

As a routine mark of punctuation, a colon is used to separate hours and minutes in expressing time.

    Ex.: 10:15 a.m.   7:30 p.m.

Use a colon in the following phrase:

    The flight arrived at 10 42 p.m.

446

Write the hours and minutes correctly in these sentences:

    A. The rapid transit bus leaves at _____ (seven fifteen) and at _____ (eight thirty).

    B. The orchestra played until after _____ (one thirty) a.m.

447

Circle the letter of the sentence that has the time stated correctly:

    A. Dwayne called at 7-20 p.m.

    B. The 9: 20 commuter bus was overcrowded.

    C. The speaker arrived at 6:25 p.m., five minutes before the luncheon.

448

Frequently, on-the-hour times are stated with <u>no</u> colon or zeros. However, in the same paragraph both even and uneven times would be expressed with the colon for the sake of consistency.

    Ex.: 1. Your orthodontist appointment is at 11.

          2. We had our choice of three flight times, which were 8<u>:00</u> p.m., 10<u>:00</u> p.m., and 11<u>:30</u> p.m.

Which sentence below would be correct?

    A. Call me at 8.

    B. The three calls came in at 10:00 a.m., 10:20 a.m., and 3:00 p.m.

449

Write the times correctly in these sentences:

    A. Where were you at _____ (two p.m.) and at _____ (four thirty p.m.)?

    B. The departures were at _____ (nine a.m.), at _____ (eleven a.m.), and at _____ (one p.m.).

Rule No. 26

The colon is also used to introduce a list, an enumeration, examples, or a formal quotation. An expression such as *the following*, *as follows*, *these*, and *thus* are commonly used to introduce whatever is to follow.

> Ex.: 1. **The three important kinds of money used in the U.S. are as follows: coins, currency, and demand deposits.**
> 2. **The following description best defines a budget: an estimate of expected income and a plan for expenditures.**

In the first example the enumeration is introduced by the words _____ _____. In the second example the words _____ _____ introduce the description.

450

Where would you place a colon in this sentence?

> Uncle Sam's money comes from the following three sources individual income taxes, corporate income taxes, and employment taxes.

451

One thing to remember about using a colon in an enumeration is that a complete sentence must <u>precede</u> the colon.

> Ex.: **There are two kinds of stock: common stock and preferred stock.**

Does a complete sentence come before the colon in the following sentences? _____
(Yes/No)

> A. The four principal types of business organizations are: sole proprietorship, partnership, corporation, and cooperative.
> B. One of the best reasons for purchasing something on credit is: to prove that you are credit worthy.

452

Circle the letter of the sentence in which a complete sentence precedes the colon:

> A. The three main advantages of a partnership include: ease of expansion, shared risk, and additional management skills.
> B. The four main disadvantages of a partnership are these: shared profits, unlimited liability, shared decision-making, and difficulty of dissolving the partnership.

453

454

To complete the sentence before the colon in Sentence A of the preceding frame, you could write the sentences several ways including these examples:

1. The three main advantages of a partnership include the following: . . .
2. The three main advantages of a partnership are as follows: . . .
3. The three main advantages of a partnership are these: . . .
4. Here are the three main advantages of a partnership: . . .

Does a complete sentence now precede the colon in each of the rewritten examples above? _____
    (Yes/No)

455

A colon throws the emphasis forward to the material following it and may be used only after a complete sentence.

The various types of banks are: commercial, mutual, industrial, and savings and loan.

Is the sentence above correct? _____ Why?_____
                    (Yes/No)
_____

456

Punctuate this sentence:

Marketing therefore creates the four basic types of utility form time place and possession.

457

Circle the letters of the sentences below which have the colon used correctly:

A. Three types of economic systems are: traditional, command, and market.
B. These are the three types of economic systems: traditional, command, and market.
C. The three types of economic systems include the following: traditional, command, and market.

458

Circle the letter of the correctly punctuated sentence:

A. A large increase in the total supply of money would have this result: It would cause an increase in prices.
B. A large increase in the total supply of money would result in: an increase in prices.

Circle the letter of the correctly punctuated sentence:

A. The three main disadvantages of a corporation are: extra taxes, special government regulations, and reduced owner control.
B. These are the three main disadvantages of a corporation: extra taxes, special government regulations, and reduced owner control.

459

The colon used in the sentence below is wrong. Rewrite the sentence so that the colon is correct:

The two principal goals of insurance are: to provide for the family and to build a reserve of funds.

_____

_____

460

You know that a complete sentence must precede the colon. Sometimes a complete sentence will also <u>follow</u> the colon. In this case the <u>first</u> word after the colon should be capitalized.

Which word in the sentences below should be capitalized after the colon? _____

A. A large increase in the total supply of money would have this result: <u>it</u> would cause an increase in prices.
B. The most important feature of insurance is this: <u>its</u> ability to provide for unexpected and very large casualty.

461

Insert and delete punctuation as necessary:

A. Remember this if savers hoarded, their money rather than invested it business couldnt expand.
B. The definition of capitalism is this the voluntary accumulation of capital, through continued savings, by individuals, to finance production.

462

Punctuate the following sentences: (Watch for review of previously learned punctuation marks.)

A. Economic efficiency means making the best use of our limited resources land labor capital and management
B. Although advertising has changed over the years its purpose has remained the same to let consumers know what producers have to sell

463

464

Punctuate this review sentence:

> Corporate bonds are considered a safer investment than stocks for this reason if a corporation fails bondholders are creditors that is they must be paid before stockholders.

465

Rule No. 27

Use a hyphen when two or more words have the force of a single modifier before a noun. Such words are called **compound adjectives**.

Ex.: 1. take-home pay
2. life-long activity

Punctuate the sentence which follows:

> Loss of income insurance is designed to replace all or part of lost income.

466

Following is a list of examples of some of the most common compound adjectives:

high-tech product	mail-order firm
long-range goal	high-priced merchandise
short-term setback	run-down neighborhood
fast-food chain	agreed-upon fee
white-collar worker	good-paying job
full-time career	medium-sized company
two-week vacation	low-level performance

Punctuate the three compound adjectives in the sentence below:

> Mail order firms have low cost operations and usually can set their prices below those of a full service retail store.

467

If the two adjectives that <u>precede</u> the noun they modify are meant to be read as a single unit, a hyphen should be used between this compound adjective.

Circle the letter of the sentence below that contains a modifier that should be read as one unit:

A. Landis was an <u>excellent</u> <u>mechanical</u> engineer.
B. We all know there is a gap between our earnings and our <u>take</u> <u>home</u> pay.

If the adjectives are <u>not</u> intended to be read as one unit, they are not compound adjectives; therefore, no hyphen would be used.

Ex.: 1. a <u>giant clearance</u> sale
2. a <u>small black</u> cat

Would the following adjectives require a hyphen? _____
(Yes/No)

a huge poisonous snake

468

Circle the letter of the phrase below that indicates a loan company that isn't large:

A. small-loan company
B. small loan company

469

Adverbs, which usually end in <u>ly</u>, are not compounded with adjectives. Therefore, no hyphen should be used between an adverb and an adjective before a noun.

Ex.: 1. high-priced products <u>but</u> high<u>ly</u> priced products
2. a slow-moving vehicle <u>but</u> a slow<u>ly</u> moving vehicle.

In the above examples high and slow are _____; highly and slowly are _____.

470

Circle the letter of the phrase that needs a hyphen (e.g., is compound):

A. professionally made ties
B. right to work laws

471

Underscore the compound adjectives in the phrases below:

a worn out shoe   a badly worn shoe
an old brown shoe   an old fashioned shoe

472

Circle the letter of the sentence which needs a hyphen:

A. A brand name is a well known name that is associated with a particular product.
B. A brand name is a commonly known name that is associated with a particular product.

473

474

Sometimes phrases can be written as a compound adjective or as a possessive.

> Ex.: 1. three-day vacation   or   three days' vacation
> 2. five-week notice   or   five weeks' notice

In the above examples the phrases in the first column are _____; the ones in the second column are _____.

475

Once again, before hyphenating, be sure the adjectives are meant to be read together as a single unit.

Underscore the compound adjective below:

an old grizzly bear   an all purpose card

476

Circle the letter of the sentence which is correctly hyphenated:

A. He wanted to follow-up the letter.
B. He wanted to send a follow-up letter.

477

Hyphenate the compound adjectives:

A. modest income families
B. single family household
C. second largest dealership
D. newly decorated home
E. home based businesses

478

Most words compounded with *well* are hyphenated when the adjectives <u>precede</u> the nouns they modify.

> Ex.: 1. a well-managed company
> 2. a well-educated person

Punctuate the following:

A. a well deserved reputation
B. a well dressed individual

Circle the letter of the phrase that contains a compound adjective:

   A. a well written report
   B. a lucrative oil well
   C. a well personality

479 ▶

Now that you have the compound adjective well in mind, remember this very important modification: If the compound adjective <u>follows</u> the noun it modifies, no hyphen will be necessary.

   Right: An up-to-date office
   Right: Our office is kept up to date

As shown above if the compound adjective (precedes/follows) the noun it modifies, (a hyphen/no hyphen) is required.

480 ▶

Circle the letter of the sentence which has the compound adjective following the noun it modifies:

   A. The analyst's view of the market was short term.
   B. Safe deposit boxes in the vaults of banks are provided on a rental basis.

481 ▶

Place a check mark beside the compound adjective in the preceding frame that would need a hyphen:

   short term   _____
   Safe deposit _____

482 ▶

Hyphenate the following wherever needed:

   A. The compliment was well intended.
   B. The Girl Scouts sold their cookies house to house.
   C. Our commute is a 35 minute ride by bus.

483 ▶

In a series of compound adjectives, the hyphen is used even when the second word of the compound is implied and placed only with the last item in the series.

484

Ex.: **The complex had one-, two-, and three-bedroom apartments available for rent.**

Punctuate this sentence:

Employees qualify for two, four, and six week vacations after every three years of service.

485

Circle the letter of the phrase that is hyphenated correctly:

A. six, seven, and eight-letter words
B. three-, four-, and five-paragraph letters

You know that:

1. compound adjectives preceding the noun *are* hyphenated.
2. compound adjectives following the noun *are not* hyphenated.
3. two separate adjectives *are not* hyphenated.
4. adverbs (ly) and adjectives together *are not* hyphenated.
5. a series of compound adjectives with the second adjective placed only with the last compound *is* hyphenated.

486

Which rules above apply to these phrases?

the Grand Ole Opry	No. _____
the dog was well behaved	No. _____
3-, 6-, and 9-cent stamps	No. _____
over-the-counter securities	No. _____
a newly formed program	No. _____

487

Circle the letters of the sentences that are punctuated correctly:

A. The procedure had become well established.
B. Aaron is the best known author.
C. A suddenly appearing storm struck violently.
D. The driver hit a high brick fence.
E. One has to rely upon day to day experiences.

488

No response is required for this frame. Please read the following:

Some words such as brother-in-law, window-shopping, letter-perfect, get-together, and double-park are always hyphenated. There are no rules to follow. The best advice is to consult a good dictionary.

You can be certain that most *self* words will be hyphenated no matter if they precede or follow the noun. (The few exceptions are selfish, selfhood, selfless, and selfsame.)

Punctuate the following sentences:

A. Self discipline is the beginning of a productive life.
B. Everyone needs a good dose of self esteem.

489 ▶

Punctuate these sentences:

A. The note should be self explanatory.
B. Selfish people aren't usually liked.
C. Please include a self addressed envelope.

490 ▶

Compound numbers *under* one hundred — between twenty-one and ninety-nine — are always hyphenated when they are written out.

Right: The gentleman was about eighty-seven years old.
Wrong: Ninety five people attended the lecture.

Why is the following not hyphenated?

One hundred fifty

491 ▶

No reponse is needed for this frame. Please read the following paragraph:

A <u>dash</u> is made by printing two hyphens together. Students frequently use a hyphen when they mean a dash. Learn to distinguish between the hyphen and the dash even though teaching the dash is not one of the goals of this text. Again, a dash is two hyphens together with no space before or after the hyphens.

492 ▶

Insert and delete hyphens as necessary:

A. Each year the Federal Reserve System clears over 25 billion checks using high speed check sorting machines.
B. A well maintained home is still a good investment if it is well financed.

493 ▶

494

Circle the letter of the sentence below that is correctly punctuated:

A. One way to spot undervalued stocks is to compare price earnings ratios to growth rates.

B. Education is becoming more and more a never-ending process.

495

Punctuate the following sentences:

A. The next best thing is a computer based model.

B. MasterCard and VISA are two of the best known all purpose cards.

496

Circle the letter to identify the sentences that are punctuated correctly:

A. The major monetary controls are legal requirements, discount rate policy, and open-market operation.

B. About one in ten Americans feels "trapped by debt"—a figure that stays relatively constant through middle- and upper-class brackets.

C. Some financially secure people regularly set aside 10 percent of their take home pay.

D. The news was covered on the spot.

497

Circle the letter of the sentence that is punctuated correctly: (Watch for review.)

A. Our connecting flight which departed at 4:30 p.m. required a two-hour delay.

B. Our connecting flight, which departed at 4:30 pm, required a two-hour delay.

C. Our connecting flight, which departed at 4:30 p.m. required a two hour delay.

D. Our connecting flight, which departed at 4:30 p.m., required a two-hour delay.

E. Our connecting flight which departed at 4-30 p.m., required a two hour delay.

498

Delete and insert punctuation marks as needed in these sentences: (Watch for <u>all</u> marks.)

A. Everyone knows this one fact: The fast-moving American economy is consumer-oriented.

B. A rule of thumb is that installment credit (excluding rent or mortgage) should'nt eat up more than 15-20 percent of ones' take-home pay.

C. Even with today's top tax rate, the dreaded income tax may reduce the work effort of some high-income people.

250

Punctuate the following sentences drawing upon all of your newly acquired punctuation knowledge if necessary:

A. Therefore AAMCO decided not to change its time honored name.

B. For more up to date information on coverage tax rates and benefits you should consult your local Social Security office.

C. In fact more than half of the US work force is employed by family owned businesses

499

Read each sentence carefully and punctuate:

A. Moran Asset Management of Greenwich Connecticut was 1987s best performer among money management firms controlling more than $100 million

B. In planning a life insurance program the familys short and long range financial needs should be determined

C. Im convinced were on the verge of a long run turnaround in farmland prices said Gregory Hanson a US Department of Agriculture farm finance specialist

500

CONGRATULATIONS!!!

You have just completed the entire punctuation text. Before taking Section Test 7, please read the following instructions; complete each step in the order presented:

1. Take Section Test 7 following the same directions given for Section Test 1. After you have inserted all marks of punctuation, turn the page and check yourself carefully, as you have been doing in the past. This self-check process is an important feature of this text. Complete the Section 7 Review Sheet, making sure that you understand all of the items that you missed on the test.

2. Consult your instructor regarding the procedure for taking the final examination.

BUSINESS LETTER

October 14 19___

Mr Rayford Skinner Jr
1604 Cravens Rd
Stevensville MI 49127-3058

Dear Mr Skinner

Grayson Inc a retail chain that sells imported leather goods plans to open 45 new stores this year many of which will be freestanding structures specifically designed for the company(E) The promise of bigger broader and better stores is part of the Boulder based chains recent efforts to present more upscale surroundings and improve its product mix said Marjorie Woolfe a divisional manager of the company(E)

In recent years Grayson has been opening about 15 new stores annually and has concentrated its growth in small to medium sized college towns(E) It currently operates 210 highly successful stores nationwide(E) Last year we purchased many successful stores around the city and now were building a prototype of how we want our stores to look Woolfe said(E)

According to long term company growth records Grayson plans to implement its store design in conjunction with affiliates of Fidelity Trust Bank(E) The company has just organized a limited partnership of which Grayson Northeast Inc and Jamestown Mortgage Corporation are the two general partners(E) Grayson Northeast is the companys Richmond Virginia regional subsidiary(E) According to Cliff Avery a Grayson senior vice president Grayson is definitely wearing the developers hat(E) We typically operate by leasing space in strip malls and we rarely own our own stores(E)

Boulder based Fidelity Trust Bank said it has agreed to lend up to $10 million to the joint venture and has so far advanced $7 million(E) During the year the specialty chain expects to open brand new stores across the country (dash) both through its stepped up expansion plans and the newly formed joint venture(E) Supposedly the Northeast is a high growth area(E)

Gary Bowers manager of six Grayson stores wants to open four new stores this year but he expects to add only about half that number(E) Bowers has said that some of his new stores will be built using Graysons prototype design and that there are definite plans to build a free standing store in Nashville Tennessee this year.

While the retail chain works to make its stores larger and more distinctive it will also introduce high quality leather merchandise to improve profit margins(E) According to the companys most recent quarterly report Grayson stands on the threshold of a long sought dream (dash) to become an international corporation(E)

Sincerely

BUSINESS LETTER

October 14, 19___

Mr. Rayford Skinner, Jr.
1604 Cravens Rd.
Stevensville, MI 49127-3058

Dear Mr. Skinner:

Grayson, Inc., a retail chain that sells imported leather goods, plans to open 45 new stores this year, many of which will be free-standing structures specifically designed for the company. "The promise of bigger, broader, and better stores is part of the Boulder-based chain's recent efforts to present more upscale surroundings and improve its product mix," said Marjorie Woolfe, a divisional manager of the company.

In recent years Grayson has been opening about 15 new stores annually and has concentrated its growth in small to medium-sized college towns. It currently operates 210 highly successful stores nationwide. "Last year we purchased many successful stores around the city, and now we're building a prototype of how we want our stores to look," Woolfe said.

According to long-term company growth records, Grayson plans to implement its store design in conjunction with affiliates of Fidelity Trust Bank. The company has just organized a limited partnership of which Grayson Northeast, Inc., and Jamestown Mortgage Corporation are the two general partners. Grayson Northeast is the company's Richmond, Virginia, regional subsidiary. According to Cliff Avery, a Grayson senior vice president, Grayson is definitely wearing the developer's hat. We typically operate by leasing space in strip malls, and we rarely own our own stores."

Boulder-based Fidelity Trust Bank said it has agreed to lend up to $10 million to the joint venture and has so far advanced $7 million. During the year the specialty chain expects to open brand-new stores across the country—both through its stepped-up expansion plans and the newly formed joint venture. Supposedly, the Northeast is a high-growth area.

Gary Bowers, manager of six Grayson stores, wants to open four new stores this year; but he expects to add only about half that number. Bowers has said that some of his new stores will be built using Grayson's prototype design and that there are definite plans to build a free-standing store in Nashville, Tennessee, this year.

While the retail chain works to make its stores larger and more distinctive, it will also introduce high-quality leather merchandise to improve profit margins. According to the company's most recent quarterly report, Grayson stands on the threshold of a long-sought dream—to become an international corporation.

Sincerely,

REVIEW SHEET

If you missed Number	See Frame Number	Practice Sentence
1	90, 100	
2	15	
3	125	
4	15	
5	15	
6	103	
7	107, 109	
8	15	
9	140, 141	
10	129	
11	15	
12	129, 245	
13	274, 275, 286	
14	468, 475	
15	245	
16	245, 248	
17	465, 467	
18	286	
19	2	
20	439	
21	57	
22	57, 59	
23	196	
24	465, 467	
25	392, 393	
26	64, 286	
27	422, 424, 425	
28	439	
29	439	
30	245, 248, 266	
31	2	

If you missed Number	See Frame Number	Practice Sentence
32	170, 182	_____
33	316, 286	_____
34	422, 424, 425	_____
35	465, 467	_____
36	2	_____
37	470	_____
38	2	_____
39	439	_____
40	170, 182, 286	_____
41	310, 313	_____
42	385	_____
43	439	_____
44	439	_____
45	2	_____
46	465, 467	_____
47	186	_____
48	422, 424, 425	_____
49	2	_____
50	286	_____
51	129	_____
52	15	_____
53	129	_____
54	196	_____
55	2	_____
56	392, 393	_____
57	103	_____
58	103, 105	_____
59	2	_____
60	245, 248, 266	_____
61	245, 248, 266	_____
62	392, 393	_____
63	2	_____
64	439	_____
65	310, 313	_____
66	2	_____

If you missed Number	See Frame Number	Practice Sentence
67	439	_____
68	465, 467	_____
69	316, 286	_____
70	2	_____
71	170, 182	_____
72	465, 467	_____
73	492	_____
74	465, 467	_____
75	64	_____
76	470	_____
77	2	_____
78	228	_____
79	465, 467	_____
80	2	_____
81	245, 248, 266	_____
82	245, 248, 266	_____
83	337, 338	_____
84	2	_____
85	392, 393	_____
86	64, 286, 316	_____
87	465, 467	_____
88	103	_____
89	103, 105	_____
90	2	_____
91	422, 424, 425	_____
92	157, 162	_____
93	465, 467	_____
94	163	_____
95	2	_____
96	392, 393	_____
97	186	_____
98	465, 467	_____
99	492	_____
100	2	_____
101	136, 141	_____

10:42 p.m.

445

A. 7:15   8:30
B. 1:30 a.m.

446

Ⓒ (Time may be expressed with or without the a.m. or p.m. Never does a space precede or follow the colon in expressing time.)

447

Both would be considered correct. (In Sentence A the reader would know whether you were referring to morning or evening. In Sentence B because the second time uses a colon and the minute, the other related numbers would have to use the same.)

448

A. 2:00 p.m.   4:30 p.m.
B. 9 a.m.   11 a.m.   1 p.m.

449

as follows
The following

◀ **450**

three sources:

◀ **451**

A. No
B. No
Therefore, a colon may <u>not</u> be used between the verb and the series that follows.

◀ **452**

B. (By using a colon in Sentence A, you are separating the verb from the direct objects.)

◀ **453**

Yes

454

No (Read the thought preceding the colon. It is not a complete sentence; therefore, a colon could not be used.)

455

Marketing, therefore, creates the four basic types of utility: form, time, place, and possession.

456

(B.) and (C.) (A complete sentence does not precede the colon in Sentence A.)

457

458

(A.)

459

Ⓑ.

460

The two principal goals of insurance are these: . . .
These are the two principal goals of insurance: . . .
The following are the two principal goals of insurance: . . .
The two principal goals of insurance as as follows: . . .
There are two principal goals of insurance: . . .
(Can you think of any more ways to write it?)

461

It   (in Sentence A)

462

A. Remember this:̲ I̲f savers hoarded,̸ their money rather than invested it,̲ business couldn'̲t expand.

B. The definition of capitalism is this:̲ the voluntary accumulation of capital,̸ through continued savings,̸ by individuals,̸ to finance production.

463

A. Economic efficiency means making the best use of our limited resources:̲ land,̲ labor,̲ capital,̲ and management.̲

B. Although advertising has changed over the years, its purpose has remained the same:̲ to let consumers know what producers have to sell.̲

Corporate bonds are considered a safer investment than stocks for this reason: If a corporation fails, bondholders are creditors; that is, they must be paid before stockholders.

464

Loss-of-income insurance

465

Mail-order firms
low-cost operations
full-service retail store

466

B. (take-home pay)

467

No   (You could say "a huge snake" or "a poisonous snake"; therefore, the words are not meant to be read as one unit.)

468

B.   (Item A indicates a company that makes small loans.)

469

adjectives
adverbs

470

B.   (In Item A professional<u>ly</u> is an adverb, not an adjective.)

471

a <u>worn-out</u> shoe
an <u>old-fashioned</u> shoe

472

A.   (In Sentence B *commonly* is an adverb and, therefore, is not hyphenated.)

473

compound adjectives
possessives

474

an <u>all-purpose</u> card

475

Ⓑ (In Sentence A *follow up* is a verb phrase rather than a compound adjective.)

476

All should be hyphenated except D.
- A. modest-income families
- B. single-family household
- C. second-largest dealership
- E. home-based businesses

477

A. well-deserved
B. well-dressed

478

479

Ⓐ

480

<u>follows</u> . . . no hyphen
<u>precedes</u> . . . a hyphen

481

Ⓐ

482

Safe deposit _____✔_____ (Safe-deposit)

483

A. None
B. None
C. 35-minute ride   (Numbers are always hyphenated when they appear with another adjective before a noun.)

two-, four-, and six-week vacations

484

B.

485

No. ___3___
No. ___2___
No. ___5___
No. ___1___
No. ___4___

486

A. (The compound adjective *well established* follows the noun *procedure* that it modifies, so a hyphen is not used.)
B. (The compound adjective precedes the noun it modifies and should have a hyphen.)
C. (Suddenly is an adverb.)
D. (The adjectives *high* and *brick* modify the word *fence* separately.)
E. (The compound adjective precedes the noun and should have hyphens.)

487

No response is needed.

488

489

A. Self-discipline
B. self-esteem

490

A. self-explanatory
B. None
C. self-addressed   (NOTE: Preferably avoid this combination. Use this instead: an addressed, stamped envelope.)

491

This number is not hyphenated because it is <u>over</u> one hundred.   (The correct way to write 125 would be one hundred twenty-five.)

492

No reponse is needed.

493

A. high-speed   check-sorting machines
B. well-maintained home   (The first compound adjective precedes the noun; the second follows the noun.)

B. (In Sentence A *price-earnings* ratios should have a hyphen because the two words modify the word *ratios* together.)

494

A. next-best   computer-based
B. best-known all-purpose

495

A. (A hyphen should be placed in *discount-rate*.)
B. (The word *middle-* is hyphenated too because the meaning is "middle-class.")
C. *Financially* is an adverb; *take-home* is a compound adjective modifying the word *pay*.
D. The words *on the spot* follow the noun *news* and therefore are not hyphenated.

496

D.

497

A. consumer-/oriented
B. should/nt (shouldn't)   ones/(one's)
C. The sentence is correct.

498

FEEDBACK

> **499**

A. Therefore, AAMCO decided not to change its time-honored name.
B. For more up-to-date information on coverage, tax rates, and benefits, you should consult your local Social Security office.
C. In fact, more than half of the U.S. work force is employed by family- owned businesses.

> **500**

A. Moran Asset Management of Greenwich, Connecticut, was 1987s best performer among money-management firms controlling more than $100 million.
B. In planning a life insurance program, the family's short- and long-range financial needs should be determined.
C. "I'm convinced we're on the verge of a long-run turnaround in farmland prices," said Gregory Hanson, a U.S. Department of Agriculture farm-finance specialist.